TEACHER'S / LEADER'S HANDBOOK

CREATIVE BIBLE LEARNING

BY ED REED
AND BOBBIE REED

FOR YOUTH
GRADES 7-12

Regal Books

A Division of GL Publications
Ventura, CA U.S.A.

The Scripture quotations unless otherwise noted are from the *New American Standard Bible*. © The Lockman Foundation 1960, 1962, 1963, 1968, 1971, 1972, 1973, 1975. Used by permission.

Abbreviations used are:

Phillips *THE NEW TESTAMENT IN MODERN ENGLISH*, Revised Edition, J.B. Phillips, Translator. © J.B. Phillips 1958, 1960, 1972. Used by permission of Macmillan Publishing Co., Inc.

MLB *MODERN LANGUAGE BIBLE, The Berkeley Version*. Copyright © 1945, 1959, 1969 by Zondervan Publishing House. Used by permission.

Fourth Printing, 1982

Published by Regal Books
A Division of GL Publications
Ventura, California 93006
Printed in U.S.A.

Library of Congress Catalog Card No. 77-76205
ISBN 0-8307-0479-5

Contents

Preface

Too long in our teaching practices we have equated teaching with telling, and learning with listening. That is not the way we learned to ride a bicycle or play the trombone. The writer of Proverbs says *train* the child. *That's* more than telling, more than teaching, *that* includes supervised practice.

Paul says living the Christian life is an active experience motivated by an inward desire to do God's will and to be conformed to the image of His Son, Jesus. Furthermore, James says the proof of the learning is in the doing.

This book is dedicated to helping teachers assist learners to discover, appropriate and practice God's principles for right living in their everyday lives.

Often as teachers we have been presented with the vision of helping learners grow in grace, but we have found that dream to be elusive, like quicksilver, when we try to grasp it. We have been challenged and found ourselves willing and ready, but soon frustrated because we have not known "how to."

Our prayer for this book is that it will be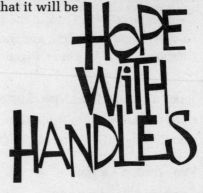

The Authors

C. Edward Reed attended Westmont College, received his B.A. in education from San Diego State University, and his M.A. in education from Point Loma College. He has taught in the public school system for 21 years, Sunday School for 25 years, and served as Junior High Coordinator at Skyline Wesleyan Church in Lemon Grove, California for the past 10 years.

For the last six years, Ed has been actively involved as a seminar leader for ICL. He has also authored *The Sunday School Teacher's Planbook—Youth, The Youth Guide Book,* and several filmstrips produced by ICL. He co-authored with Rex Johnson, "Bible Memories," a game built on recognition of Bible characters.

Bobbie Reed attended Arizona Bible College. She has taught Sunday School, worked with Vacation Bible Schools and Bible clubs, and co-sponsored youth groups for 16 years in several churches across the United States.

Bobbie is currently Director of Staff Development for one of California's state agencies, and is completing her Master's degree in Public Administration at California State University at Los Angeles, teaching at Coastline Community College in Fountain Valley, California, and serving as Managing Editor for *SOLO*, a Christian magazine for single adults.

Bobbie has also written Junior High and Adult curriculum for Gospel Light Publications, written for *TEACH* magazine and co-authored books for ICL *(Bible Learning Activities—Youth, Your Sunday School Can Grow).*

Foreword

The International Center for Learning is committed to obeying Christ's command to "Go...make disciples...and teach" (Matt. 28:19,20, *Phillips*). To fulfill this great commission, ICL provides in-depth training for leaders ministering in churches of all sizes. ICL helps teachers discover how to motivate students to be involved in learning the life-changing truths of God's Word.

Since 1970, thousands of Sunday School teachers and leaders have attended ICL Seminars and Clinics. Repeatedly, teachers express a strong need for training, a desire to improve their abilities to teach God's Word. The response of these teachers to the ICL program has been enthusiastically positive.

This book is designed for both the new teacher and those who are more experienced. Ed Reed and Bobbie Reed concisely present the needs and characteristics of youth. They will help you discover a variety of ways you can provide effective Bible learning. These insights into your learners, the learning process, and appropriate methods and materials will enable you to make the Bible come alive for your learners.

You can profit from reading this book alone and discussing it with a group of teachers. You will want to refer to this book many times for assistance in planning new methods and programs as well as improving what you are already doing. Also consider using the book as a part of an ongoing training program for staff members in the youth division of your church.

We trust that this book will help you as you obey Christ's command, "Go...make disciples...and teach."

Lowell E. Brown

Lowell E. Brown
Executive Director
International Center for Learning

PART 1

LET'S LOOK AT THE BASICS

THE CHALLENGE

WHAT YOUTH NEED TO GROW

A FRESH LOOK AT LEARNING

The Challenge

Charles, the youth division coordinator in a local church, was visiting in the home of Steve and Carol. He was sharing with them the challenge, excitement and vision for ministering to youth as they considered becoming a part of the youth teaching team.

"Yes, God has always been looking for teenagers who would be willing to follow Him," Charles repeated for emphasis. "I am reminded of Joseph who was determined not to sin against his God, of David who believed that God was in control in every situation and of Josiah who led his nation back to God. Then there's Daniel, Shadrach, Meshach, and Abed-nego who trusted God in small things so that when the larger tests came there was no hesitation in their obedience. I think of Mary, who in complete trust submitted her future to God.

"Paul instructed Timothy to be an example to others in his youth and he repeatedly offered himself as an example for Timothy to follow. He made that an open invitation when he wrote the church at Corinth, 'follow me even as I follow Christ.' Our young people are no different. They need more than instruction. They need models too. That's really why I'm talking to you. We feel that God has laid you on our hearts and we'd be glad to have our young people follow you."

"That sounds pretty scary," Carol sighed.

"A big responsibility," added Steve.

"Yes," Charles answered, "but exciting too."

THE EXCITEMENT

Charles continued, "Teaching them how to win in their daily walk with Jesus is exciting. And to hear about their victories over sin and self is really thrilling."

"I'm not sure I could tell them how to do that in a way that would make sense to them," Steve continued.

With a gentle chuckle Charles replied, "We really don't want you to tell them."

"You don't?" Carol asked incredulously. "I thought that's why you were here."

"Let me explain," Charles answered, "A few years ago I had an opportunity to take a group of young people to a music festival in Hawaii for a week. No matter how I tried to describe what we would see and do in Hawaii (I had been there before), I never saw my excitement and expectations mirrored in their eyes. Frankly, I was somewhat disappointed.

"But my excitement returned and turned to joy when I saw their excitement as they snorkeled with the tropical fish in Hanauma Bay, screamed during the water fights in the outriggers, and braced themselves against the torrent of wind at Pali Lookout late at night. I remember thinking then how pale my verbal descriptions on the mainland a month earlier were compared to the reality of being there.

"Telling young people about the wonders for successful living to be found in God's Word is much like those pale descriptions. How much more fulfilling it has been to lead them to where these wonders can be found, and to make it possible for them to experience the joy of discovering those wonders for themselves."

"That does sound exciting," said Carol.

"Could you give us an example of that from teaching?" Steve asked.

"Sure," Charles smiled. "Take Mike, for example. He hadn't been a Christian very long. I remember the Sunday the Junior High Department had been studying how we ought to treat non-Christians. Their discoveries had been written on the chalkboard when Mike interrupted the silence that followed with 'Oh I understand now.' "

" 'Understand what, Mike?' the department leader asked.

" 'My brother and I share an early morning paper route,' Mike continued, 'Last week he was sick and I did it by myself. I just figured this week I'll sleep in and he can do it. But that's wrong. See that third point on the board—do things for them without expecting anything in return? If I want to show God's love for my brother I should do the papers for him and not expect him to do it by himself this week. And I won't either!'

"You can be sure that more than one teacher *was moved by Mike's discovery.* It's really neat when God lets us see a bit of the vision He has for these learners."

THE VISION

"When Jesus saw fields ready for harvest in John, chapter 4 He saw people ready to receive eternal life. He looked at Peter and saw in him a potential to be immovable for God—a rock, one who would not crumble under the pressure of the Jewish Council in Acts, chapter 4. He saw quite a different Peter from the blustering, impetuous, vacillating fisherman-disciple, who occasionally showed sparks of spiritual brilliance.

"We see teens today who are not unlike the 'old' Peter. Many are blustery, impetuous, vacillating. They suffer from poor self-concepts, and feelings of inadequacy and insecurity. But when we look beyond to visualize the stable, patient, loving, strong, and mature sons and daughters of God that can be their inheritance, we see fields white unto harvest as Jesus did."

THE OBJECTIVES

"That's a beautiful vision," commented Steve thoughtfully. "Are there some specific objectives you hope to reach with the program of your youth ministry?"

"Yes, there are five I would like to share with you," Charles replied earnestly.

1. Providing for Spiritual Growth

"It is important that we provide an environment where young people can grow spiritually. Because they need both spiritual food and spiritual exercise for proper growth, we design our teaching plan to allow for:
  a. discovering spiritual principles from God's Word;
  b. discussing how spiritual principles apply to life situations;
  c. making plans to use those principles in their own lives;
  d. practicing and sharing the results."

"The spiritual exercise of making specific plans to use God's principles during the week and then actually doing it ought to provide quite a bit of good spiritual exercise," mused Steve. "That sure makes a lot of sense."

"It certainly would be easier to understand James' perspective on problems if they use some of them in their own lives," laughed Carol.

"By the way," Charles continued, "our goal is not simply that young people understand spiritual concepts and principles. We also want learners to make a personal decision to live by God's values as they are presented in the Bible. Just because I think something is important does not insure its value to someone else. You've heard about the young person who goes off to college only to lose his faith? And we wonder, was it really his faith that he lost or was it his father's faith, his pastor's faith or his Sunday School teacher's faith?

"Consider the blind man in John 9. In spite of the fact that his parents folded under pressure from the Pharisees when asked about their son's healing, the ex-blind man boldly proclaimed, 'Jesus did it.' Not too surprising when you consider it was his own faith and not his parents'. We want to be sure our young people have thought through what it means to follow Jesus and, like the blind man, are willing to declare their faith.

"This transferring of values to young people is not usually a quick process. However, our style of teaching makes knowing where our learners are in the transition not only possible but probable." (See chapter 2 for further discussion of transference of values.)

2. Service

"A second objective is service," continued Charles. "Involving youth in service is a joyous experience for a teacher. It is the outcome of teaching God's Word with positive results. Usually it's as easy as pointing them in the right direction and watching them take off! What is not simple is finding that 'right direction.' Investing lives in service deserves at least as much careful thought as the investment of money would.

"Opportunities for service are as many and varied as the needs of our world. Christian teen-canteens, coffeehouses, musical festivals, operating a community recreation facility with a Bible story hour, or running a summer child-care center for working mothers are only a beginning. You can name at least a dozen more practical, worthwhile projects if you'll use your imagination a little. Don't forget to ask your young people for their ideas—you can bet they'll have a few!

"One consistently successful endeavor many youth groups choose is planning and conducting a rural VBS for one or two weeks during the summer! Being responsible for lesson and craft preparation, doing door-to-door visitation, and shouldering the burden of reaching children for Christ are exciting experiences for youth. The eternal rewards for it are theirs. They earn them and they know it. Whatever sacrifices they make, however often they are tempted to give up, when it's over, the joy of service repays them for their personal involvement. What greater goal would you set than this, to serve the Lord with gladness?"

3. Outreach

"A third goal is to reach unsaved people for Christ. Students can do this through some of the projects we just mentioned. They can also bring unsaved friends to many of our youth activities. Furthermore, we design our teaching times so that we can effectively include newcomers and so that it is possible for them to participate in the session."

4. Fellowship

"And then there's fellowship. All of us need fellowship." Both Steve and Carol grinned and shook their heads in agreement. "Our youth need to have fun in a Christian context. If we don't provide opportunities for them to express that part of their natures, we may communicate, 'If you want to be spiritual come with us, but if you want to have fun look to your worldly friends for companionship.' "

"Oh, no!" exclaimed Carol in horror, "I never thought of it quite like that."

"And yet," Steve reminded Carol, "didn't that same idea present a lot of problems for us as we grew up?" Carol nodded her head.

5. Meeting Needs

"Our fifth goal, but by no means the least important, is that of meeting the individual needs of the young people. Needs vary widely from student to student. Every student needs to be affirmed, to be called by name, to be made to feel an important part of the group, to have someone who will listen to his ideas and thoughts, to have someone who will help him think through how to handle problems, to know there is someone who cares for him.

"Our ability to help young people with these needs will begin with our ability to accept them as they are, not as we wish they were. Jesus first called His disciples servants, then friends and later brothers. He allowed them to grow and change, to succeed and fail and He affirmed them at each stage of their relationship. We try hard to accept young people as Christ has accepted us."

THE TEACHER'S CALL

Let's leave Charles' conversation with Steve and Carol for a few moments to explore an often asked question in depth. How does one know that he is called to be a teacher of youth? In fact, how can one be sure of a calling to any task in the Church? If a person could be sure that he was called, he might depend more on God's ability to equip him. Just what is a "call"? Does one hear a voice calling him as Samuel did or have a vision like Paul on the Damascus Road?

First, there are certain basic principles. One of these principles is that we are all called to be disciples of Jesus Christ, follow Jesus as both Lord and Saviour. That call includes the idea of discipline, of being obedient to God's will. Obedience means the desire to know what God wants you to do, to know what area of ministry He wants you to be involved in. Obedience means that you start moving toward that area of ministry, open to any changes that He might want to make.

In your search, you will find lots of help! The visitation committee is certain that you are the only one they need to help them in their work. The nursery department is convinced that they need you most. The pastor says he sees in you the qualities needed for a deacon. The youth minister feels confident that you could best be used in the area of teaching youth.

However, if all these opportunities are available, how can you know which one is God's choice for you? Who is right? How can you decide? This certainly is not what is meant by a call! It is more like mass confusion. How can you move from your willingness to obey Christ to a sure knowledge of the area of ministry that God has for you?

Paul seems to have anticipated this problem as he describes the church as the Body of Christ. He speaks of this in several places (see 1 Cor. 12; Eph. 4; Rom. 12:3-8). If you are to understand your area of ministry, you need to see the interrelationships within the Body of Christ.

Just as there are two eyes, two ears, a nose, two feet, four fingers and a thumb on each hand in our physical body, with each working in a different way, so also in the Body of Christ there are a variety of gifts or ministries.

In the three passages previously listed, you will find about eighteen gifts, depending on how you divide several of them. These are not talents, like playing the piano or singing, but are "ministries." Some of these are sign-gifts, such as the gift of tongues, of interpretation of tongues, miracles and healing. For our purposes here, we will limit our discussion to the other gifts, the gifts of service. These include pastors, evangelists, giving help, showing sympathy, administration and teaching.

Along with the principle of variety, there is also a universal distribution of these gifts in the Body of Christ. Every Christian has been given a spiritual gift. If you have received Christ into your life as Lord and Saviour, then you have been given a spiritual gift of service! This gift of service is your "calling!"

But the question still remains—"How do I find my calling?" We have just changed the wording so that we now ask, "How do I find my spiritual gift?"

Discovering Your Spiritual Gift

Let us first look at Romans 12:3-8. As Paul introduces the subject of spiritual gifts in this passage, he begins with the admonition to make a "sane estimate of your capabilities" (Phillips). You begin by looking carefully at yourself. Several options for service are open. You can serve on the visitation committee, work in the nursery, be a deacon, or teach youth. Paul says that the first step is not to look at the options, but to look at yourself and your abilities. How has God put you together? What would you really enjoy doing? Be honest! Not "What ought I to do?" But "What would I really enjoy doing?" Your work in the Body of Christ should be an offering of joy, an act of celebration, not some drudgery that pushes you to the edge of nervous collapse.

Note that nothing has been said about being qualified. That is not the question at this point. You begin by evaluating your feelings and abilities to find out where you would enjoy serving. Along with this step you find out what would be involved in each choice. In other words, you make an effort to be more familiar with all of the facts. If you feel drawn to working with youth, before you make that decision you should do some observing of the youth programs, talk with some other adults working with the youth department, and find out from the youth minister what will be expected of the person taking this position. Perhaps even a trial run at helping another teacher might be arranged.

Along with investigating and observing, pray that God will guide you in your choice.

The second step in discovering your gift is in verse 6. "And since we have gifts that differ according to the grace given to us, let each exercise them accordingly." If in the process of evaluation, observation, investigation and prayer, you feel that you would enjoy teaching youth, then the next step is to start teaching. You tell the youth minister that you are available to begin. But just as in physical exercise, you do not go all out the first time. You need training. So you study and start learning all you can about teaching youth. Start by serving as a substitute or assisting another teacher. Or you may learn by "in-service training" by taking a class of your own. With the help of the department leaders, you will quickly be able to assume full responsibility as a teacher of youth.

Once you have moved out in faith by exercising what you believe to be your gift, the third step is the confirmation of that gift by the results. These "results" are hard to define. It might be the response of the class to your teaching—the encouraging comments that you get from individuals in the class. It could be numerical growth. Or it may simply be the sense of satisfaction that comes after the class session—the satisfaction that it was a good session with lots of involvement by the students and good discussion that says you are "coming through."

What if there is no confirmation? What if you find total frustration? Make sure that your frustration does not come from a lack of training, or from failure on the part of the departmental leaders to clearly define your task. But if everything has been right and you still do not find this confirming result, then move back to the first step and reevaluate. Stepping out in faith sometimes includes making mistakes. Do not hesitate to correct these mistakes and move on!

At long range, your spiritual gift will be confirmed when it accomplishes the purpose of spiritual gifts; "equipping of the saints for the work of service, to the building up of the body of Christ" (Eph. 4:12). The spiritual gifts are given to all of God's people in order that they be able to minister. Spiritual gifts are given to equip youth for their work in God's service, to the purpose of the building up of the Body of Christ. This is why we teach youth. The purpose is cyclical. We teach youth so that they mature to the point of teaching others and finding their place of ministry in the Body of Christ. We are trying to help each other attain "to the unity of the faith, and of the knowledge of the Son of God, to a mature man, to the measure of the stature which belongs to the fulness of Christ. As a result, we are no longer to be children, tossed here and there..." (Eph. 4:13,14). This is the goal of the learning process in Christian education.

Exciting Fulfillment

What are the results in your own life as you find your spiritual gift of service? There is a sense of adequacy. You now understand how God can equip you for the job He has called you to do. It is a "spiritual" gift—the Holy Spirit is at work in and through you.

Sometimes we think that the Holy Spirit is looking for empty vessels. So we sit around trying to empty ourselves. We empty our heads waiting for the Holy Spirit to fill in the blanks. But the Holy Spirit is looking for *fit* vessels! As you discover and exercise your gift, you become fit to be used by the Spirit of God. You become fit by doing all you can in preparation, confident that the Spirit will saturate all your efforts with His power. This gives you confidence. And when you are confident that you are in the place God has for you, and that His Spirit is at work in you, you can be a "real" person, honestly growing and learning with your students.

It is a glorious and awesome calling, to be a teacher. If God has appointed you to be a teacher of youth, then exercise that gift in the boldness of faith and in the confidence that God will equip you for the task.[1]

SOME LAST THOUGHTS

As Charles concluded his description of the objectives, Steve looked at his wife and moved a little closer to her. Placing his hand in hers, he said, "We'd like to be a part of that kind of ministry to the youth in our church." As they paused for prayer, Charles thanked God for their openness to His Spirit.

If you are already ministering to youth in Jesus' name, this book is for your help and encouragement.

If, like Steve and Carol, you are not yet involved in a teaching ministry, we would like to ask you a very personal question.

Are you open to God calling you to minister to young people, to be an under-shepherd of His flock? If the answer is yes, this book is for you. It is meant as a "how to" book for those who are willing to share God's truth with young people in a teaching ministry.

And if, as you read on, you find that God is filling your heart with a desire to share His love and guidance with young people, it may well be that Jesus is asking you as He once asked Peter, "Do you love me?" When Peter said yes, Jesus simply said, "Feed my sheep."

FOOTNOTE ■ Chapter One

1. David A. Stoop, *Ways to Help Them Learn* (Glendale, CA: Regal Books, 1971), pp. 47—51.

What Youth Need to Grow

"And then..." Jim paused dramatically for emphasis, "Tom looked me straight in the eye and said 'But, Mr. Smith, I thought that was what you'd expect from a 13-year-old!' "

Bob and Jean laughed appreciatively at the story, and Kay, Jim's wife, nodded her head, remembering the incident which had occurred just last week in the Bible study session for eighth graders she and Jim taught.

"Tom could never have spoken out that way two years ago!" Jean said thoughtfully, remembering how quiet Tom had been in the sixth grade class she had taught. "It never ceases to amaze me how kids can change so much when they get into junior high!"

"That's what makes teaching young people the most exciting challenge anyone could ever ask for!" Jim leaned forward, his eyes shining.

"Oh, no!" groaned Kay, "you've got him started again. We'll be here all night!" But she blew him a kiss and went to the kitchen for more coffee. In spite of her teasing, she loved the kids as much as Jim did.

FROM CHILDREN TO ADULTS

The transition from being a child to becoming an adult involves some of the most significant life changes a person ever experiences. A youth often questions values that were superimposed on him by parents and teachers. And that questioning compels him to rethink, wrestle with and redecide values he has presumed were his. During this time every aspect of life and every idea, emotion, relationship, habit and interest a young person has is affected. The post-adolescent person is as different from the preadolescent as the butterfly is different from the caterpillar!

When planning sessions for youth, a teacher will want to be aware of and take into consideration the age level and developmental stage of his learners.

No two learners develop at the same rate, but there are some general expectations of and differences between seventh and twelfth graders. These are illustrated in the following chart:

FIGURE 1 ■ **Characteristic Differences Between 7th and 12th Graders**

Characteristic	7th Grader	12th Grader
1 Thinking process	Thinks in concrete, abstracts are difficult. Teacher needs to use specific examples of abstracts (e.g., Abraham offering Isaac).	Able to think in abstracts.
2 Reasoning	Finds principles and concepts difficult to deal with.	Handles principles and concepts well.
3 Time to complete an assignment	Takes approximately twice as much time as a 12th grader. Teacher must plan session to allow enough time.	Works approximately twice as fast as 7th grader, so teacher can schedule more and more complex Bible learning methods.
4 Questions	Fact questions are easy, but "why" questions are often difficult (although worthwhile). Teacher must write questions carefully.	Able to make deductions from a series of facts.

Characteristic	7th Grader	12th Grader
5 Discussion	Generally answers and contributions are superficial. Teacher must be prepared with a series of questions designed to probe and assist the junior highers in peeling off the superficial layers, to get to the core of the issue.	Able to discuss issues in depth.
6 Verbal Reporting	Easily distracted by a look or a snicker from the group. Thus the learner needs written notes from which to make his verbal presentation so he can successfully share his discoveries.	Confident with verbally expressing ideas to group.
7 Sitting still	Finds it difficult to sit for extended periods of time. Teacher must plan enough movement and breaks.	Able to sit for extended periods of time (but this doesn't ensure attentiveness!).
8 Interest	Needs to be actively involved in the learning process, so use effective Bible learning methods.	Needs to be actively involved in the learning process, so use effective Bible learning methods.
9 Motivation	Is concerned with "What's in it for me?"	Concerned with "Who else is doing it?"
10 Emotions	Is relatively unstable in feelings, and attitudes can change quickly. A teacher may find that one day the kids love him, and the next they can't stand him! The important thing is to be constantly loving toward them.	Is relatively stable in feelings and attitudes. Tends to be slow to change.
11 Attitude toward opposite sex	Not much interested in the opposite sex.	Very interested in the opposite sex.
12 Spiritual expectations	One step at a time, please!	One step at a time, please!

Remember that your learners will grow at different speeds in different areas. Some will shoot up physically like weeds, and we are sometimes disappointed when they do not act emotionally as grown up as they look! Also, some seventh graders may surprise us with their spiritual insight and maturity, while some twelfth graders may be spiritual babes and we must content ourselves with baby steps!

It is important to find out what each learner's battles are and to help him plan to win using God's power principles. Expectations or visions of spiritual growth possibilities will vary from young person to young person depending upon the individual. Some will respond quickly as did Peter and John. Others will come later as did Nicodemus. If we are faithful in the sowing and watering of the Word in the lives of our learners, God will bring the increase and harvest in His time.

PHYSICAL NEEDS ARE IMPORTANT

As young people mature physically, they experience a series of physical changes which are alternately fascinating and irritating to themselves and others. This period of physical maturation is marked by several changes other than the preparation of the body for reproduction. The body growth of the large muscles is quite rapid; yet, the development of coordination is slow. So, unaccustomed to his new body, the teen often bumps into things, falls down, and generally needs a lot of room to move around. His growth produces an explosion of energy which he must use, and often he just can't sit still for long periods of time.

The aesthetic sense of a young person develops because his eyes mature at adolescence and because he also has a heightened sensitivity to light and colors. So, you will want to make use of vivid visuals in your teaching ministry to further stimulate a teen's response and learning.

In fact, you will want to create a total classroom environment which will provide youth the physical comfort they require for the maximum learning opportunity. Therefore, as a teacher, you will want to check these things before each session:

- Is the room temperature comfortable?
- Is there good ventilation?
- Are the table and chairs the right size?
- Is there enough walk-around space?
- Is the classroom lighting good?
- Is there enough or too much sunlight coming through the windows?
- Are blinds or curtains needed?
- Is the room dark and depressing, or cheerful and inviting?
- Are the room acoustics as good as they could be?
- Will the learners be able to hear you and each other?
- Can the chalkboard and visual displays be seen from every chair in the room?
- Have you planned a variety of Bible learning methods which will involve the learners physically?
- Have you planned enough breaks in activities for learners to move around?
- Is there a drinking fountain nearby?
- If you are planning for a long session, consider providing nutritious snacks for quick energy.

In order to be as effective as possible when planning for learning, a teacher also needs to take time to understand the other major developments and challenges facing his teenagers and realize that change is a gradual process. Often adults become anxious and impatient with the rate and direction at which a teenager develops. When the adults' expectations are not realized, conflict results. Consider Cheri's situation. Her parents expect her to keep her room picked up daily, but Cheri feels that once a week is more than enough. So, Sunday through Friday, mother and Cheri argue the issue, sometimes automatically, sometimes bitterly. By Saturday when Cheri does clean her room, Mother's frustrated response may well be, "It's about time!"

In other words, the difference between what parents and teachers expect and what a teenager does is the measure of tension and anxiety in the home or classroom!

To reduce the tension, both the young person and the adult will need to rethink their expectations, face each situation as it really is and go from there. Often a workable compromise is possible! If both Cheri and her mother would agree that the room would be cleaned up twice a week, the arguments, tension and frustration would probably be reduced.

Reducing tension and frustration will often open communications and improve relationships. Anyone who wishes to communicate effectively with young people *absolutely must* accept and keep in mind that every person is an individual and will develop at his own rate and in his own time. No two young people will ever develop in exactly the same way, at the same time or at the same rate. And, to expect them to is unrealistic and can result in a teenager's feeling inferior, having a poor self-image, and developing a bitter spirit.

Let us consider four different ways that young people grow and develop.

GROWING TO SEXUALITY AND SINGLE RELATIONSHIPS

As young people mature they develop an awareness of their own sexuality. At the same time they are also moving from group relationships (relating to guys and girls in a general way) to single relationships (forming friendships with guys and girls on a one-to-one basis).

We all have social needs for fellowship, conversation, working together, loving and being loved, sharing our feelings and having others share their feelings with us. In addition to these needs, teenagers have special social needs. The development toward sexuality and the forming of single relationships result in a teenager's redefining his social interactions.

Sometimes a teen develops more in one of these areas than in another. Jim may be developing friendships with individual girls and guys, but feels very uncomfortable with the sexual feelings, urges and emotions he is experiencing, even to the point where he may refuse really ever to accept his own sexuality. Unless he does, he will find it difficult either to give or receive in a marriage relationship.

FIGURE 2

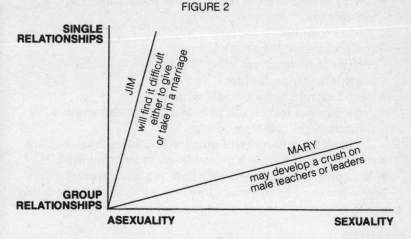

On the other hand, Mary may fully accept her sexuality (all the feelings and emotions that are beginning to emerge), but has not yet developed the ability to relate to guys her own age. Yet, she sees in the male youth teacher everything she's looking for in a husband: someone who would provide spiritual leadership, be protective, meet her needs and not take advantage of her. Because she does not find these qualities in guys her own age, Mary is likely to develop quite a crush on her male teacher! The youth leader who is aware of what is really happening, can do great services to the "Marys" of his world by redirecting those attentions toward building good relationships with young men in their peer group.

In the illustration, both Mary and Jim need further growth.

Social Interaction

Because appropriate interaction with peers is essential to growth, a teacher must carefully plan the session and how social interactions will occur. When a learner is uncomfortable socially he is less apt to learn. Therefore, as a teacher, you will want to check these things before each session:

- Have I planned Bible learning methods which will allow learners to...
    - work together?
    - discuss what they have learned?
    - share their feelings?
    - get to know each other?
- Have I established a climate which...
    - encourages learners to love and accept one another?
    - discourages criticism of others?
    - allows for difference of opinion and even disagreement?
- Am I making friends with my learners as individuals?
- Am I promoting a group spirit among the learners?

If you answer yes to these questions, then you are probably providing appropriate social interaction for your learners.

GROWING TO SELF-IDENTITY AND LOVE

The second area of development leads from family identity to self-identity and from selfishness to love.

We are not born with a concept of self. An infant has no concept of his own personal identity. He is unaware of where his body ends and the environment begins.

A child is aware of having personal wants and desires which frequently are opposed to parental wants and desires. But, a child has not yet really developed an awareness of his own identity either. He identifies himself in relationship to his family, friends or grade level. "I am a fourth grader." "I am Joey's friend." "I am a Johnson."

The adolescent begins to struggle through the development of a self-concept which adequately answers the question "Who am I?" The struggle often shows in the rebellion against authority and tradition, in the intense questioning of ideas and values, and in the identification with or admiration for famous or important people.

At the same time that the teen is developing his self-concept, he should also be moving from an attitude of selfishness to a position of self-acceptance and love. This task involves a teen's learning to accept himself as he is and learning to accept others as they are. Jesus tells us this. "You shall love the Lord your God with all your heart, and with all your soul, and with all your strength, and with all your mind; and your neighbor as yourself" (Luke 10:27). Yet, we cannot truly love others until we have learned to love ourselves. One neat thing about being a Christian is that we can go to God and ask Him to help us make needed changes in our lives to make us more lovable (Christlike).

Sometimes an adolescent will develop more in one of these areas than in another. Linda may learn to love herself and others, but never develop a self-identity which is separate from her family ties. She may remain "tied to her mother's apron strings," as the saying goes.

FIGURE 3

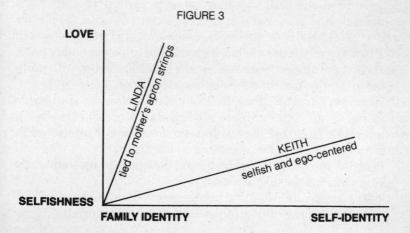

Keith may have a very definite self-identity, but may not have really learned to love himself and others. Keith will probably be very egocentric and selfish in his relationships. Both Linda and Keith need further growth.

This growth to a personal identity and to real love may be the most stressful phase of an adolescent's development. The struggle between the desire for self-identity, "It's my life. I'll do it my way!" and the need for love and approval, "How am I doing, Mom?" often tears him apart.

Individual Affirmation

Because a wise teacher will want to assist the teenager in his development, he will want to communicate acceptance and a sense of personal worth to the learner through individual affirmation. A teen uses significant others in his life as mirrors to evaluate his own personal value. He will begin to increase in self-esteem when he believes that others value him as an individual. The more value he senses that others place on him, the greater his self-esteem and acceptance grows.

There are many ways to communicate personal value to learners. Being attentive, supportive and encouraging, and calling a learner by name will say that he is important to you. Jesus communicated personal worth to Zacchaeus by going to dinner at his house (see Luke 19:1-8). He communicated personal worth to Peter by envisioning what he would become (see John 1:42). Jesus communicated personal worth to Nathanael by affirming his character in the presence of his friends (see John 1:47).

Whatever a teacher does that communicates to the learner his personal value, will facilitate the learning process. Likewise, a learner, who feels that the teacher is not personally interested in him, is less likely to be interested to learn.

Plan for building self-esteem and acceptance by frequently asking yourself these questions:

■ Do I listen attentively to my learners when they share?
■ Do I affirm the efforts of the learners as appropriate?

■ Do I plan Bible learning methods which encourage learners to share insights and understandings?

■ Do I allow individuals to express their ideas and viewpoints honestly and openly?

■ Do I avoid overpowering the learner when his view differs from mine?

■ Do I encourage a nonjudgmental attitude on the part of the learners?

■ Do I discourage my learners from belittling each other, but rather encourage a supportive fellowship?

If so, you have probably provided a good climate for your learners to grow in the area of self-identity and love.

GROWING TO INDEPENDENCE AND SELF-DISCIPLINE

The third area of adolescent development leads from dependence to independence and from parental discipline to self-discipline.

We all begin life totally dependent on others for food, transportation, shelter, clothing, pleasures, guidance and discipline. This is normal and acceptable in a child, but totally unacceptable in an adult! During adolescence, most people move from a position of dependence to one of independence. At the same time, they grow from requiring parental discipline toward exercising self-discipline. In our society we expect "well-balanced adults" to have developed an appropriate amount of self-discipline for the amount of independence they exercise.

One of the great problems of growing up is that the teenagers do not usually grow toward responsible self-discipline and independence at the same rate.

Nancy may be very self-disciplined and consequently very dependable when it comes to following instructions and keeping commitments. But she may never have developed independence and does not exercise her own initiative or make decisions for herself.

FIGURE 4

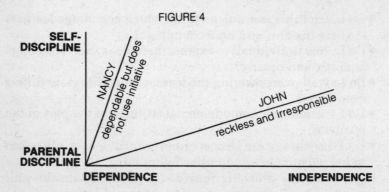

On the other hand, John may be quite independent and capable of taking all kinds of risks. But he may not have learned self-discipline. Thus he seems reckless and irresponsible. Both Nancy and John need further growth.

Frequently adults and teenagers disagree bitterly as to which comes first, independence or self-discipline. The teenager often says: "Give me independence and I will develop responsibility later." The adult usually says: "Show me responsibility and I will feel comfortable giving you more independence."

FIGURE 5

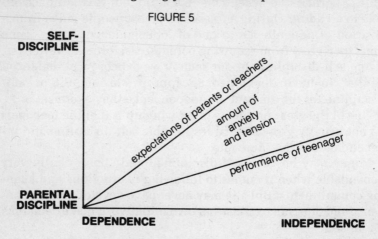

These differing demands can become the basis of tension and anxiety. The farther apart they are, the more tension can be predicted. Either the adult or the teen can reduce the tension by reducing his demands. However, rather than expecting the adult to change, it is frequently easier to persuade the young person to make the first move. You can assist many of your teens in their growth by showing them that the quickest way to gain more independence (without tension) from the adult, is through voluntary submission to the adult's expectations (to show the adult the responsible self-discipline he expects).

As young people exhibit more self-discipline and gain more independence, you as a teacher should notice a difference in their learning styles. They should begin to assume the increased responsibility for learning God's life principles and they may amaze and delight you with their creativity as they express their faith.

Design Learning for Growth

All of your learners should find excitement and stimulation in challenging Bible learning methods. However, those teens who are developing self-discipline and independence usually find a special fulfillment in Bible learning methods which allow for creative expression.

Before your next teaching session, answer these questions:

■ Have I planned Bible learning methods which will encourage learners to...

think analytically?
explore new ideas?
make personal evaluations?
try new roles?
reach meaningful goals?
develop as individuals?
be creative and innovative?

If you have, your learners will probably find their learning experience to be fun and fulfilling.

THE KEY TO DISCIPLINE

A teen's growth to independence and self-discipline is important to understand if you want to have effective discipline. Good discipline in the classroom is not just "sitting still" or "being quiet." It is control of behavior from within. The teacher and learner work together in a team relationship—the teacher providing guidelines and controls from without and the learner trying to exercise responsibility within—so that maximum learning can take place. Someone has said that discipline, simply stated, is "making good disciples." Becoming a disciple of Jesus Christ requires obedience and self-discipline in every area of life—"taking every thought captive..." (2 Cor. 10:5); "I discipline my body and make it serve me..." (1 Cor. 9:27, *Berkeley*); the discipline of relationships—"He who loves father or mother more than Me..." (Matt. 10:37); "Those whom the Lord loves He disciplines..." (Heb. 12:6).

The big question about discipline in Christian education is how can we effectively maintain it? Here are some suggestions that may help us answer that question.

A Teacher Can...

1. Accentuate the positive. We are quick to call attention to negative behavior. How quickly and often do we reinforce positive behavior? "I really appreciated how you..." "You're really good at..." are two statements that can greatly affirm your learners. Actively look for opportunities to affirm not only problem learners but also those learners who have already mastered self-discipline. Furthermore, don't dwell on the wrong a student has done. Rather, accentuate the positive he should do next time instead.

2. Be sure the rules are clear. If the students know and clearly understand what behavior is acceptable and what behavior is unacceptable, you will have laid a good foundation for self-discipline within the classroom. Rather than a long list of dos and don'ts, you might try the one rule: You may do anything you like as long as it does not interfere with the learning of others or endanger anyone's physical safety.

3. *Rules must be realistic.* Do not expect your learners to exhibit behavior not consistent with their maturity. If it is difficult for them to sit still for long periods of time, redesign your teaching time to include periods of activity. The more you know about your learners the more you can help them in this area. Furthermore, do not expect them to do what you are not willing to do. For example, if you expect them not to talk during a worship time, be careful not to talk to another teacher during that time, etc.

4. *Enforcement of discipline must be consistent.* Nothing can undermine your credibility any more than, "This is the last time that I'm telling you for the last time." If you have indicated that the next time John disturbs the class you will talk to his father, you had better follow through. There is great security for your learners in knowing where the boundaries are.

5. *Recognize the cause of the problem.* Generally there are three causes for discipline problems:

(a) *Facilities*—too stuffy, too cold, too crowded; poor lighting; not enough Bibles; inadequate supplies to do the project; too noisy. These factors can trigger discipline problems, so be alert to the learning environment and seek out practical solutions or alternatives.

(b) *Bored*—more involvement on the learner's part will usually cure this.

(c) *Problem oriented*—usually it is a problem the learner has brought with him that is the cause, not a problem generated in the classroom. It may be that the learner is forced to come by his parents. Your learner may have come in already disturbed about special pressures from peers, parents, school, authorities or friends. A family showdown over proper attire for church can be upsetting enough to a teenager to destroy the will to learn and cooperate in class. Individual counseling between teacher and learner can be a key in this situation.

6. Be a name dropper—when you sense that a learner is tuning out, or is beginning to engage in distracting behavior, use his name in the middle of a sentence. When their name is heard students will automatically zero back in on you, and you have not had to stop what you are doing to get the desired effect.

7. Ask a question of the person whose attention you wish to re-engage. Be careful to remember to state the question first and then the name so that the other learners will also consider the question.

8. Sit next to the disturber or between two who disturb the class. This can be most easily handled when you are seated in a circle.

9. Be a toucher. This can be a "touchy" subject with many people, but when done with discretion and common sense, touching can be a very effective tool for discipline: Much problem behavior is an attention-seeking device. A gentle touch on the arm, shoulder, etc., can communicate both a great deal of personal affirmation and gentle correction on a nonverbal level. You will probably feel more at ease doing this if you are a man teaching boys or a woman teaching girls.

10. Spend time outside of the classroom with the student. This provides a good opportunity to get to know students better as well as a chance to ask about specific problems. "I noticed that you seemed to be having a hard time in class this morning. Is there something bothering you that we could talk about, pray for, etc. Help me understand how I can help you better...."

When disciplining remember to do everything possible to encourage positive, self-discipline. An unprepared teacher is more responsible for problem behavior than are the learners. An undisciplined leader can expect undisciplined learners. An overpowering dictator can count on rebellion and scheming to break down the self-discipline of the class—after all, if he is going to carry all the responsibility for order, why should they control themselves?

Are you teaching youth to discipline themselves? Or merely

punishing them when they do not, thereby increasing the outer discipline rather than the inner?

A Department Leader Can...

1. *Be alert* to discipline problems developing.

2. *Stand beside* the offender while listening to the class.

3. *Try a gentle touch* on the shoulder while standing by the learner.

4. *Join the class* by pulling up a chair next to the learner.

5. *Ask the learner to talk* with you outside of the class circle.

6. *Ask the learner to share* with you what seems to be bothering him/her. This allows the class to continue uninterrupted while you are helping the problem learner.

7. *Make a decision*—either return the learner to the class; give the learner an optional assignment; try a one-on-one class, you and the learner.

8. *Follow up in the home.* Be careful not to condemn the student to the parents, but rather to ask for ways that you or the teacher can help their teenager. There are two factors here:

(a) When you attack a child, psychologically the parents feel attacked.

(b) When asked for help, a parent tends to become more open about what is going wrong at home, school, etc., and many times you can form an effective partnership with the parent in helping the teenager.

9. *Encourage and affirm learners* whenever possible. Remember to emphasize what students do right and help them understand how they can grow to self-discipline and maturity.

GROWING TO A VALUE SYSTEM AND A RELATIONSHIP WITH GOD

The fourth major area of development for a teenager leads him from conscience to building a biblical value system and from religion to a relationship with God. During his adolescence a person often reevaluates or redefines his faith, values, concept of God, religion and conscience. This is, perhaps, the one area of growth which parents and teachers find most difficult to accept. We respond as if a teenager who is allowed to question the reality of God will lose his faith!

The sobering truth is that for many teenagers (and some adults) there has never been a transference of ownership of faith. That is, they have never moved from believing because "someone else" says it is true to being able to say "I believe because *I* believe it's true." Until this transference has occurred, the faith isn't really theirs to depend upon or act on.

Philip had been a Christian since he was 10 years old. He could easily quote biblical principles for most situations. He had heard these from the pulpit and in the Bible study sessions for years. But, because Philip never really owned his faith for himself, he ran into trouble when he went away to college. After several confrontations with his atheistic philosophy professor, Philip reached for his faith and it was not there! Whose faith had he lost? His pastor's faith? His parents' faith? His Bible study teacher's faith? Or, was it his own?

"That which is mine, of value to me, I do not easily let go of." (Anon)

We see many illustrations of superimposed values in the home. Truths or values "superimposed" by parents but not "bought" by their children account for many of the changing life-styles which we notice when some teenagers finally leave home. While under the authority of the parents, the teenager is likely to appear to conform to the parents' values. The more the teenager conforms to these values the less friction there seems to be between parents and teen. Likewise, when the parents' values are either challenged or disregarded you can usually count on more friction. Many teens, preferring less friction at home, agree within themselves at least temporarily to play by their parents' rules. The same thing happens in the spiritual realm. Parents and teachers cannot expect their values (no matter how noble they may be) to be perpetuated in the lives of their children and students until there has been a transference of those values.

When does transfer occur? Transference has occurred when the child has "bought" the values for himself. The word "buy" is appropriate here because it always costs to adopt God's values. It may cost a number of things, including selfish desires, but as one teen said to her father, "It is important that the value be valuable to me. It needs to be a part of me—not just a rule."

What makes a thing valuable? Usually the value of an item is determined by the amount a person has to invest in order to make it his. The more a person invests, the more valuable it becomes to him. Once someone has invested in an article, an idea, or a relationship, it becomes something that he will protect and defend.

How protective are our young people of what they have been taught? Do they defend their beliefs or desert them when the pressure comes? What kind of value do they place on maintaining their relationship with Jesus and following Him in obedience? Sometimes we may feel that our youth know the truth, but that they do not place high value on it yet.

So the questions come: How can we help our youth value the truth we teach to the extent that they use it? How can we help them value their relationship with Jesus above all their values?

Modeling by Investing

First and most important, we cannot transmit values we do not possess. We ourselves must value our relationships with Jesus above other values. Why should young people invest in something that is not valuable to us? When our relationship with Jesus is important, we invest in it with time, energy, money, thought and courage and we reap spiritual dividends proportional to our investment.

Values are more caught than taught. So when teachers who are investing in their relationship with Jesus also invest in young people, spiritual dividends show up in the lives of the young people. They watch—and catch—because they are looking for worthwhile values!

Encourage Them to Invest

Secondly, we can help our young people invest, much as a trust officer at a bank might help a young person with his investments. Junior high youth will be willing to invest of themselves if they can see a worthwhile reward at the end of their investment. Of course they decide what is worthwhile to them, so a wise teacher elicits suggestions from his young people. Camping trips, parties, ball games and other social events are usually motivating enough to elicit investment in Bible study, service, discipleship and even outreach.

High school youth are usually less motivated by extrinsic rewards than by the approval of other youth and significant adults. So if people who are significant to them are investing in their relationship with Jesus, they will be caught up in the tide.

This suggests a strategy for ministry to high school youth. It starts with a teacher or a group of teachers who become significant persons in the lives of a few high school youth as they invest in these youth. Then the teachers disciple the students until the students value their relationships with Jesus more highly. Third, the teachers help their disciples invest in the lives of other high school youth. The effect is one of multiplication, and it is scriptural (see 2 Tim. 2:2).

Investment Currencies

Time is something most young people can readily invest. They will probably never have as much time as they have during their junior and senior high years. But if the time they commit is spare time, it is not as much of an investment as priority time would be. So priority time invested in worship, ministry, fellowship, discipleship or outreach will bring bigger dividends in terms of changing values.

Energy is another investment currency for young people.

Working at something until one's bones ache is a "valuable" experience for young people.

One group of young people worked almost all night setting up an outreach ministry to the community of Avalon on Catalina Island off the coast of Southern California. They have already forgotten a lot of other things they have been taught, but they still remember that night vividly—and many of them "reevaluated" their commitment to God that night!

Thought is an investment most teens will be glad to make if they can think with someone. Of course, if problems posed to young people are only rhetorical or memory problems, or if the "right" answers are too obvious, they will avoid them. But young people are willing to invest thought in more complex problems, especially if they can explore Scripture and discover practical and personal solutions that are applicable to them right now.

Money is an area of investment for young people, believe it or not! The fact that they do not have much money to invest makes what money they do invest all the more valuable. Personally oriented projects attract investment because the results are quickly obvious.

Possibly the best kind of investment for helping young people value their relationship to Jesus is that of courage. If a teen will take a stand for Jesus in the face of peer pressure, it will be either because he values that relationship with Jesus already or because he values his relationships with others who are also taking a stand. In either case, taking a stand will help him invest even more.

Of course, if a stand takes too much courage, young people will lie low. They may want to be courageous, but see the cost as too high. So a good place to start is to ask teens to take a stand right in class on relatively less important issues, and then support them extensively. They need you on their side.

As Jesus said, "For where your treasure is (values are), there will your heart be also" (Matt. 6:21).

A Balance Is Needed

As teenagers build a biblical value system, they should also be developing a personal relationship with God. As these two goals are reached, youth build stability and spiritual maturity into their lives.

Sometimes, however, a teen grows more in one area than in another. Tom may have developed a relationship with God based on feelings and emotional responses, but never have taken time to learn and value the biblical instructions and principles for Christian living. Tom will be unstable in his daily walk.

FIGURE 6

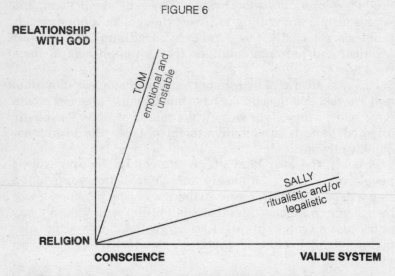

Sally may have totally owned the biblical values and principles and may follow them scrupulously. But if Sally does not develop a vital, personal relationship with God, she will become a ritualist and/or a legalist (a modern-day Pharisee). Both Tom and Sally need further growth.

You will want to ask the Holy Spirit's guidance in stimulating your learners to spiritual growth.

Spiritual Growth

The key to providing opportunities for spiritual growth lies in carefully seeking the Holy Spirit's guidance when planning the Bible study session. Ask that each individual learner will receive the personal understanding and insight he most needs and is ready to accept. Then before the session, check your plans:

- Have I planned Bible learning methods which allow learners to explore God's Word and to discover truths for themselves?
- Can I listen to serious doubts about any aspect of the Christian faith without feeling threatened? If it does not threaten God, why should it threaten me?
- Do I encourage the learners to share with me honestly?
- Have I planned for learners to develop a relationship with God rather than an acceptance of "religion"?
- Will I ask learners to share how they will apply the Bible truths in their lives during the week?
- Do I know how I will handle difficult spiritual questions which I may not know how to answer?

When you can honestly answer yes to these questions, you will probably have planned a climate which will be conducive to spiritual growth for your learners.

THE EXCITING CHALLENGE

Just as with most other exciting challenges, working with young people has its difficult times. The only thrill greater than watching a child become an adult whose life is submitted to God's direction, is being actively involved with the young person in that process! And that, a good teacher knows, is more than just his responsibility. It is also his exciting privilege!

Before moving on, take one last look at the youth you work with. Read the chart on the next page. Jot down names of youth you know who fit these descriptions. List some of the implications for your teaching and youth work.

The **10-year-old** is self-contained, relaxed, direct, easy in his give-and-take.

Eleven is more tense, questing, and egocentric; he searches and tests his self by conflict with others.

Twelve is in better balance; accepts others; sees both them and himself more objectively; but unevenly fluctuates from childish to more mature attitudes.

Thirteen withdraws and inwardizes in order to focus more deeply upon his own thoughts; moods and images in a manner reminiscent of **Seven.**

Fourteen, more outgoing, seeks and defines his self by comparing it with others, by matching and by imitation; he is less inwardly centered.

Fifteen withdraws not physically but mentally to meditate, and to explore his self in relation to ideas, ideals, and the opinion of others.

Sixteen is more at ease and circulates more freely among age-mates and adults; seems more independent and self-reliant.

■ ■ ■

This condensed, thumbnail gradient enables us to see the growth of the self in fuller perspective. Although the day-to-day growth may be quite imperceptible, the year-to-year progressions are unmistakable. There is an uninterrupted advance from concrete to conceptual attitudes and from naive egocentricity to a perceptiveness of the selves of others. With the aid of the culture the mechanisms of maturation assist the adolescent in his searches to find himself.[1]

FOOTNOTE ■ Chapter Two

1. Arnold Gesell, Frances L. Ilg, and Louis B. Ames, *Youth: The Years from Ten to Sixteen* (New York, Harper and Row, 1956), pp. 355–356. Used by permission.

NOTE SPACE

A Fresh Look at Learning

Mark hurried into class several minutes early one week. "Guess what?" he demanded excitedly of his small group teacher, Pete.

"Must be something great!" Pete smiled at the boy's enthusiasm.

"I did it! I really did it! What we talked about last week. You know, about getting angry at Tom? Remember I said I would try returning 'good for evil?' " He stopped to catch a breath. "Tom started in on me again Monday, like always, and I began to get angry. I was ready to hit him right in the stomach, just like I did the last time. Then I remembered my plan and caught myself just in time. I gave my anger to God. And then I offered to return Tom's library books for him. Was he surprised! Then he said why didn't we walk over together 'cause he had to go that way anyway. We sort of got to know each other, and would you believe it? He's coming over tomorrow and we're going swimming together!"

Pete put his hand on the boy's shoulders and gave him a quick squeeze. "Sounds like you really learned something last week! I'm really glad for you!"

LEARNING IS...

Have you ever wondered how to determine if real Bible learning is taking place in your Bible study session? Some of the most faithful teachers "teach" every week of the year, but their learners never show a single sign of having "learned" what the teacher is teaching.

The true criterion of Christian learning is not just obtaining Bible knowledge, but being able to follow and put into practice the teachings of the Bible. Teachers tend to assume that they have taught and a learner has learned if the lesson has been covered. Not so. We must teach so that some kind of change occurs in the life of the learner. This may be simply the acquisition of new knowledge or it may be a change in his attitude or his behavior. But some kind of change must be effected before we can say with assurance that the learner has learned.

Let us take a look at four elements of an effective Bible study session that work together to make Bible learning effective.

THE WORK OF THE HOLY SPIRIT

For teaching to result in genuine life changes, both teachers and learners must give the Holy Spirit His rightful place in the learning process. We are seeking to teach and to learn spiritual truths, not just intellectual facts. We are also seeking changes in our attitudes and behavior which come only from strong inner motivation. The Holy Spirit is the only Person who can motivate genuine and permanent life changes. "But the Helper, the Holy Spirit, whom the Father will send in My name, He will teach you all things, and bring to your remembrance all that I said to you" (John 14:26).

One teacher relates the following experience that vividly illustrates the Holy Spirit's role in the learning process.

One Sunday after a study of the Good Samaritan story, the students were to apply the principles learned in the Bible study to a contemporary situation. "A new girl in school, of foreign extraction, whose dresses are too long, and who makes A's in math and science finds that the other girls have cut her off and won't be friendly. OK, Judy Christian, what would you do?"

There were lots of comments during the small group discussion, and then it was report time. Rhonda stood up hesitantly to report for the group. "We know this isn't the answer you're looking for, but," she continued with downcast eyes, "we're not going to get involved. We're afraid of losing our friends, too."

There was a heavy silence in the room. The teacher gulped, and thanked Rhonda for her honesty and willingness to share. There wasn't any need to straighten them out because what they really had said silently was, "We know this isn't the Jesus way, but this is where we are. Can you accept that?"

The following Wednesday night in Bible study the students watched a film that paralleled the story line of that first open-ended story to the letter. Rhonda was in the teacher's discussion group. They laughed about the coincidence and then the teacher asked her if anything had changed since Sunday morning.

"Funny you should ask," Rhonda replied. "I couldn't get away from what we had said. I wrestled with that for quite a while and then I said, 'OK, God, send me someone new to school so I can be their friend!' "

Rhonda wanted a chance to prove that she really had had a change of attitude and commitment. The teacher could never have applied enough pressure to bring about that kind of change. But, the Holy Spirit knew exactly how to do it in such a way as to help Rhonda grow.

The Holy Spirit uses God's Word in a powerful way to change lives. The more we can bring students into direct contact with God's Word and help them to wrestle with the Holy Spirit about its meaning, the more exciting, life-changing learning will occur.

Consider your teaching a moment. Do your students hear God's Word secondhand because you are always telling them what God has taught you? Or do they encounter the power of God's Word firsthand and directly interact with the Bible and the Holy Spirit?

FIGURE 1

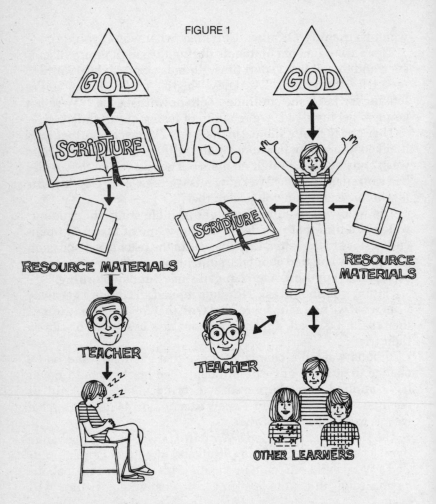

Allow the Holy Spirit to be an active, powerful part of your teaching. Include Him in your planning. Talk with Him about specific learner needs. Encourage students to talk with God about their responses to His Word and about their personal needs.

GOOD TEACHING METHODS

Teachers need to use effective teaching methods to encourage real learning and life changes on the part of learners. Through observation, study and testing, Christian educators are learning more about the entire learning process and how it works. What factors are involved in learning? Is the learner really learning what he is being taught? How much do teaching methods influence learning? What results can you expect from different teaching methods? The following are some factors to consider as you try to plan effective teaching methods.

1. Active involvement is better than passive listening. Both secular and Christian educators who have studied the results of different teaching methods are discovering that a learner learns infinitely better when he is actively involved in the learning process, as opposed to when he is only passively listening.

For example, remember your first biology course where you sat through lecture after lecture on the internal structure of the frog? You listened and you took notes, but all those scientific names just sounded strange. Then finally one day the teacher led you to the biology lab where you had to cut open a frog for yourself. The teacher walked quietly around the lab observing first one student and then another. Sometimes he would look over your shoulder or ask you a question or point out something you missed. But he never took over your exploration. He wanted you to experience and discover the inside of a frog for yourself. And do you remember how that one afternoon in the lab with your very own frog had a more lasting effect on your memory than all the biology lectures put together?

Now let us go back to our Bible study session. Has not much of our Bible teaching been more like the biology lectures than the afternoon in the lab? Many teachers have taught their lessons by "telling the Bible story" while their learners sat and listened. The teacher was active, and the learner was passive.

When Jesus fed the 5,000 with the boy's lunch, He asked the

disciples to pass the food out to the people sitting on the grass. Imagine the impression it made on the disciples to handle the food and see it multiplied before their eyes. Jesus not only allowed the disciples to observe Him walking on the water, but He invited Peter to walk with Him. When Jesus turned the water to wine in Cana, He had the servants fill the waterpots for Him. Because they had filled pots, and knew that those pots contained only water, the miracle had a greater impact on them.

2. *Variety and appropriateness* are keys to remember. Jesus often used lecture, but He varied the length to fit the occasion. And He used, as often as possible, objects (i.e., water, bread, sheep, vine) which left indelible impressions on His hearers' memories. He also taught through conversation and through asking questions which made His learners think for themselves. Jesus gave His disciples, or learners, opportunities to be actively involved in the learning process. Consider the appropriateness of His methods, and note the variety in the types of parables, illustrations and situations Jesus used for teaching.

3. *Organized* learning is the most effective learning. Choose your methods and materials so that learning is an orderly process. We will talk more about how to do this in chapter 4.

4. *Provide for feedback* Many teachers use methods which never provide the opportunity to know if the learners really heard correctly what was said. A momentary distraction, preformed opinion or misunderstood word can cause a learner to incorrectly interpret what a teacher or the Bible is saying.

FIGURE 2

Effective Bible teaching methods will allow for the student to tell the teacher both what he has understood the Bible passage to say and his own ideas on how to apply those Bible principles to life situations. That way the teacher can correct any wrong ideas or misunderstandings while the student is still in the Bible session.

5. *Learner needs* are an important consideration in planning effective teaching methods. How often teachers tell students that the Bible is exciting and life-changing and that God cares about student needs...by giving a long dull lecture? How many students are told that Christians are to be friends but never have time to talk with other students and share ideas during class? It was once said, "The brain can only absorb what the seat can endure." Good teaching methods will convey both verbally and experientially that learning is fun, meaningful and meets needs. Remember, your student has physical, social, mental and emotional as well as spiritual needs. All of the needs must be met for truly effective teaching.

THE ROLE OF THE TEACHER

In the "traditional" classroom the teacher is seen as actively telling and the learner as passively receiving. However, when the learner is actively involved in the learning process, the roles of both teacher and learner change.

Teachers who are now realizing that *they have not taught until the learner has learned* are asking questions like "What should the learner be able to do at the end of our study?" "What life changes will show that he is really learning?" "How can I lead my learner into his own personal discovery of God's truth?"

Today's educators know that a learner learns in direct relationship to how much he experiences himself, like the student in the biology lab. So, both the teacher and the learner are active now. The teacher is active as one who guides, stimulates, models and cares. The learner is active as one who receives information, explores, discovers, appropriates and assumes responsibility.

First, let us look more closely at the teacher's new roles.

One Who Guides

Relying on the indwelling Holy Spirit as the source of all spiritual teaching, the Bible study teacher guides his learners into stimulating learning experiences.

In teaching which involves the learners, the teacher is like a mountain-climbing guide. All the climbers have the same goal—to reach the mountain peak. The guide plans the journey and finds the best routes for climbing. The group then follows the guide's directions. Some members of the group may climb well, while others are slowed by the difficulty of the climb or by lack of skill. But they stick together and help each other and as they work to reach the goal together, they become a "team."

A good teacher guides his learners in much the same way. First he considers the individuals in his small group and their special needs. Then he selects aims (learning goals) for the session—something which every learner can do by the end of the session (something reasonable and reachable). Then he decides which learning methods will best help the learners reach the goals. Some of the skilled learners will be able to grasp the spiritual truths easily, while others may find them more difficult to understand. But as the faster minister to the slower, and as the teacher encourages, affirms and guides the learners, a great spiritual bond is fused and they approach the goals together.

Instead of guiding and allowing the learners to climb for themselves, some teachers tie their "mountain climbers" together, blindfold them and then try to drag them all up the path. With this method the group rarely reaches the peak, and seldom do any of the learners develop their own climbing skills. The teacher who uses this method usually fears that some learners will get lost or fail if he allows them any freedom. However, an alert teacher-guide can prevent learners from wandering or failing by giving direction or redirection through the use of questions or additional instructions. This way he still allows learners the freedom to discover for themselves, but guides them to the right answers.

The old adage, "Never tell someone anything he can discover for himself," fits even the Bible study session. But many teachers are afraid to let their learners explore the Word of God for themselves. They fear their learners will make mistakes or draw the wrong conclusions. To avoid this danger, the teacher goes to the Bible, wrestles with the biblical concepts and studies additional research materials. When he has discovered the answer, he returns to the group and tells them his conclusion. This method of teaching denies the New Testament doctrine of the priesthood of every believer to go directly to God and to learn for himself. It also denies the power of the Holy Spirit to lead each learner to the true understanding of Scripture.

When the teacher decides that it is better to be a guide, he may find it very difficult at first to make the transition from *one who tells* to *one who guides*. Most teachers use the teaching methods that were used by their own past teachers, and so they continue to perpetuate passive learning practices.

One way to make the transition easier is for a teacher to expose himself to effective involvement learning situations, like those provided at the International Center for Learning seminars and clinics. These seminars and clinics will not only provide opportunities for teachers to experience involvement learning, but also help teachers to plan (under the guidance of the seminar leaders) involvement learning for their youth.

Experiencing a "participation" class in action will also help teachers realize how much more learners learn when they are free to explore together (with the teacher there to guide and point them in the right direction).

One Who Stimulates and Motivates

A good teacher will try to motivate his learners and make learning exciting and fun for them. He will raise questions to which his learners will want to find the answers and he will learn how to guide them into learning with this method. He will plan to involve the learners actively in the session, and to use the class-room environment creatively.

Furthermore, a good teacher will remember that what motivates one student may not motivate another. This means that as he plans he will need to provide a variety of topics, questions, styles of teaching and activities over a longer period of time. He will carefully select his teaching methods, keeping his learners' needs in mind. For example, he might ask a group of girls to write an entry in Moses' diary telling what happened on Mount Sinai. However, he would ask a group of boys to make an entry in a log or journal, or to write a newspaper article (be-cause most boys would not be motivated to write a diary).

Finally, the teacher who wants to stimulate and motivate should remember that enthusiasm is caught, not taught. His own enthusiasm about the meaningfulness of God's Word and his own excitement for the learners to learn for themselves are two of the strongest assets he can have.

One Who Models

The most important thing in the teaching process is not what a teacher says, but what kind of person he is. Robert F. Mager, a well-known writer in the field of education, says, "Recent re-search has confirmed the fact that when you teach one thing and model something else, the teaching is less effective than if you practice what you teach."[1] How true this is in Christian educa-tion! Jesus and Paul each emphasized the importance of a teacher being a living example of his teaching. Jesus said, "A pupil is not above his teacher; but everyone, after he has been fully trained, will be like his teacher" (Luke 6:40). Paul said he and his fellow workers lived as they did "in order to offer ourselves as a model for you, that you might follow our exam-ple" (2 Thess. 3:9). He also said, "Be imitators of me, just as I also am of Christ" (1 Cor. 11:1).

The teacher makes a commitment to the lives of his learners. It is a commitment to be an example as well as a communicator of God's truth. Babies learn by imitation, and they imitate the people they spend the most time with—usually their parents. The same thing is true of spiritual babies. They imitate their spiritual elders. The best teacher is one who does not limit his time with learners to Bible study session time, for they need opportunities to observe and then imitate his example in everyday situations.

Moreover, if the teacher wants his learners' lives to make an impact on their world of school, business, home, or whatever, the teacher must ask himself what kind of impact he is making in his world of everyday opportunities and responsibilities. The teacher cannot ask nor expect his learners to live beyond what he is committed to himself.

One Who Cares

Think back to those teachers who most influenced your growth as a Christian. What stands out most about them in your memory? What they taught you? Most people say, "It's the fact that they cared for me as an individual."

Jesus modeled the life-style and goals He taught, but He also showed love for His disciples. He had dinner at Matthew's house and at Zacchaeus' house and with the tax collector's sinner friends. When Peter's mother-in-law was ill Jesus visited in the home. He frequently accepted hospitality in the home of Mary, Martha and Lazarus. He also took His disciples with Him as He went from place to place. They spent time with Him when He was teaching the multitudes and also when He withdrew alone to pray. They were with Him when He was transfigured and also when His Spirit was distressed in Gethsemane. They learned from being with Him and by observing His behavior in the good times and the bad times.

Jesus' disciples knew that Jesus was not just teaching them truth or training them for ministry. They knew that they were His personal friends and that He truly loved each one of them. Jesus said to them, "I have called you friends, for all things that I have heard from My Father I have made known to you" (John 15:15). Jesus considered His learners His friends, and Bible study session teachers need to follow His example.

When a teacher really cares for his learners, he will be their friend and arrange to spend time with them. He will be available to his learners, not just on Sunday, but also during the week. And he will share his life with them—both victories and struggles. Furthermore, as teacher and learners together face their struggles in faith and mutual dependency upon Jesus Christ, their love for each other will grow.

THE LEARNER'S ROLE

Now let us take a look at the learner's role in a Bible study session where he is actively involved.

Receiving Information

There are two kinds of information the learner receives in a Bible study where he is an active participant. He receives instructions telling him what he is to do in the learning process. Read, list, describe, discuss, illustrate are some of the key words that will be used. He may answer questions, discuss problems, illustrate ideas and a variety of other activities. These instructions need to be clear, step-by-step and achievable if he is to succeed in learning.

The second type of information he receives is what is often called lesson content. This may come through teacher explanation or lecture, reading the Bible, discussing with other students and the teacher—any process whereby he receives new information or reevaluates the meaning of things he has known before. Learners are always receivers of new information. The important questions are: What information are they receiving? Are they receiving that information in the most effective way possible?

Exploring and Discovering

The active learner needs to do some of his own investigation on the subject he is studying. He may examine a Scripture passage, use research materials to study the meanings of words or cultural background of passages, or answer questions related to the passage. The important thing is that he thinks and explores for himself under the guidance of the teacher. This way he learns the Bible truths firsthand and learns that he has personal access to the teaching power of the Holy Spirit.

This exploration may occur alone or in a group as he works together with others. The point is ... the student is the explorer.

One boy had been working on an assignment for several minutes when suddenly he jumped up and yelled excitedly, "I've got it! I've got it!" He had figured out something he had not known before, and he was excited about it. It was his own personal discovery, just as if no one else had ever found it before. A truth becomes truly personal when the learner has discovered it by exploring on his own. That is called the joy of discovery!

This exploration and discovery process is something which may overlap and recur several times in a given study. A student explores a Bible passage, discovers Bible principles to the life of a teenager, re-explores the Scripture passage, and then discovers applications which are especially meaningful for him.

Appropriating

According to Webster's Dictionary, appropriating is making something one's own. Once the learner has discovered Bible truths and possible applications of them, it is important that the teacher help him decide on specific ways he can "make those truths his own." What can he do in the coming days to put them into practice?

Assuming Responsibility

A learner is assuming responsibility for the truth he has discovered when he *begins to act on it* and make specific life changes as a result of his discovery. Just because a learner explores for himself, discovers previously unknown truth and even sees the personal implication of it, does not insure he will do anything about it. Remember Mark from the beginning of this chapter? When he put his plan not to fight into action, he was assuming responsibility for what he had learned.

To change life patterns is difficult and sometimes painful, and we often resist even when we know our old way is wrong. When a learner rejects change, a good teacher starts the learning process over again and prays for the Holy Spirit to intervene in the learner's life. Complete learning has not really occurred until the learner demonstrates he has changed his thinking, attitudes or actions to conform to the Bible truth he has discovered.

As a guide, the teacher may help the learner plan what steps he will take to initiate and implement needed change. The teacher may provide the opportunity for the learner to take those steps, but the learner himself takes the action and assumes the final responsibility for learning. It is as the learner changes in response to the Holy Spirit's prompting that he is in the process of being conformed to the image of Christ.

NO SHORTCUTS

There are no shortcuts to genuine learning. The teacher must guide, stimulate, model and care. The learner must receive instructions, explore, discover, appropriate and assume responsibility. This kind of learning requires both time and patience, but it also produces change in learners' lives and that is exciting!

FOOTNOTE ■ Chapter Three

1. Robert F. Mager, *Developing Attitude Toward Learning* (Palo Alto, CA: Fearon, 1968), p. 63.

PART 2

LET'S GET ORGANIZED!

ORGANIZING YOUR LEARNERS

ORGANIZING YOUR TEACHING TIME

ORGANIZING YOUR FACILITIES

Organizing Your Learners

"All right! I see the need to get my students involved in the learning process instead of listening to lectures and sleeping. And I think I know several people who will help me teach so we can have smaller groups. But what do I do now? We've always had all of our seventh through twelfth graders together in one large group. I've just never thought of doing it any other way. How do I suddenly break them into smaller groups? Who goes in which group?" Gary threw his pencil down in frustration.

Gary was facing a problem that most youth leaders face at some time or another: How do I organize my learners most effectively?

Selecting an organization plan must be individual to each church for maximum effectiveness. Let us take a look at some basic principles of organization which may help you organize your learners for more effective involvement Bible study.

SEPARATE JUNIOR AND SENIOR HIGH

Most Sunday Schools have major age-groupings (divisions) of Early Childhood, Children (grades 1–6), Youth (grades 7–12), and Adult. These may vary slightly, but they tend to follow the groupings in your local school system. However, these groupings are still too large. There is a tremendous difference between the average seventh and twelfth grader, and having them together in one group can make a difficult learning situation.

The average seventh grader is squirmy (boys), giggly (girls), inept at social relationships, uncoordinated, thinks mostly about food, and usually thinks mostly in concrete terms. The twelfth grader thinks about dating, college, future jobs and marriage. He is capable of longer attention spans, can handle abstract thoughts and deeper conversations and tends to be very impatient with the immaturity of junior highers. Therefore, if at all possible, separate your junior high and senior high students into two groups.

CLASSES—THE BASIC LEARNING UNIT

The most basic learning unit is the small group which consists of three to eight learners and a teacher. The group needs to be large enough for peer interaction, but also small enough so that each learner will have ample opportunity to be actively involved and receive individual attention.

It is difficult to involve more than eight learners at one time. However, some classes may need to remain even smaller. For example, eight active seventh grade boys in one group is probably too many.

If you are one teacher working alone with more than eight learners, students still need to work at times in smaller groups (three to six) where it is easier to share. These times will be more effective if a teacher guides the small group sharing, but you may need to adapt until teachers are available.

The following are some considerations to keep in mind when grouping students into classes:

1. Consistency Builds Depth

In some Bible sessions several teachers work together to handle a larger number of students. When breaking this "larger" group into classes during the session, it is most effective if students are in the same group with the same teacher for a series of sessions.

If the teacher desires a greater depth of sharing and honesty during the Life Exploration and Conclusion-Decision part of the session (see chapter 5), trust must build among students. This takes time. Having consistent groups will allow this trust to build over a series of weeks together. Furthermore, it is easier for a teacher to build relationships with students if he sees the same three to eight students session after session for several weeks. Finally, if a student makes a commitment to apply a Bible principle in a specific way during the week, it is easier for a teacher to follow up on that commitment if he sees the student the following week in the class.

2. Grouping by Grade

Youth are in the process of rapidly changing. There is a great difference between a seventh and ninth grader and between a tenth and twelfth grader. Because of this, it is often beneficial to group students by grades, or by two grades. Three grades, especially if those three grades are from seventh to ninth, make a large span of age characteristics within one group. Here are some options.

FIGURE 1

A	7 8 9	10 11 12	
B	7 8	9 10	11 12
C	7	8 9	10 11	12
D	7 8	9	10	11 12
E	7	8	9	10	11	12

Again, keep in mind the division of grades in your school system as you form class groups. For example, if all of your ninth graders attend junior high schools and all of your tenth graders attend high schools, you will not want to use plan B because the tenth graders may resent being held back with the junior highers.

Also remember, students have a need to meet others and feel a part of a larger group. You will want to have activities where all of your junior highers and all of your senior highers are together so they develop a sense of identity as part of the larger group.

3. Guys and Gals

Educators wrestle with the pros and cons of grouping learners into single-sex or coed groups. Youth need to interact with learners of the opposite gender if they are to build wholesome Christian social and spiritual relationships. A good youth program will provide these opportunities regularly. However, there are some considerations which indicate that single-sex class groups are a wise idea.

Pretend you are a tenth grade boy. You are in a class group and opposite you is sitting a girl you have been wanting to date. The lesson is on temptation and the teacher asks, "What temptations are especially attractive to you?" You know that you have been having a lot of struggles with your thought life and the conversations in the locker room are not helping. That is really the biggest problem in your life, but when it comes time for you to share, what will you do? Share it and risk losing the respect of that gal you like? Not answer the question? Talk about someone else's problem? Share a lesser problem like the temptation not to study?

Now think of yourself sitting with a group of guys and encountering the same question. Would you find it easier to share what is really on your mind?

A group of senior high boys were asked by a visiting teacher how they would have felt if there had been girls in the small discussion group during the sharing time. There was some nervous laughter. Then a basketball player who was also president of the youth group replied that it would not have been nearly so open and honest a discussion if there had been girls there!

Guys find it difficult to be open and honest about spiritual problems in front of girls. They really have too much to lose by taking off their "masks" in the presence of girls they would like to be accepted by. And girls find it equally difficult to express their secret hopes and fears in front of guys, especially since many of those hopes and dreams relate to dating. Youth need to grow by discussing and exploring where they are hurting and what they are fearing...in a safe environment. This happens best when small group membership is all of the same sex.

For these reasons, it is wiser to mix grades within a class group while keeping it single-sex rather than mixing sexes. In other words, more openness can be achieved if you have seventh and eighth grade boys in the same class group and the seventh and eighth grade girls in a different class group than if you have seventh grade boys and girls in one group and eighth grade boys and girls in the other group (assuming you can only have two groups).

You may not agree with this concept of single-sex grouping in class groups at first, but if after a time you find that your learners are not sharing at a deep personal level during Life Exploration and you still have both sexes meeting together in the same small groups, try single-sex groupings for a quarter and see if things do not change!

(NOTE: Be sure to select teachers of the same sex to lead the single-sex groups so they can serve as role models, empathize with the learners, and provide security for the sharing.)

You may be wondering how to meet the need to be together with students of the opposite sex during the learning time if you have single-sex class groups.

USE DEPARTMENTS

A group of learners and teachers who are all working *together* to achieve the same objectives using the same curriculum is called a *department*. (This may not be your definition of department, but for the sake of discussion use this definition throughout the rest of this chapter.) Thus a department may be comprised of one or more classes.

If you have that seventh and eighth grade boys' class and that seventh and eighth grade girls' class meet in the same room and work together to achieve the same objectives using the same curriculum, you now have a department. You have met the need for students to be in a single-sex group. Yet because the two classes are working together, you also meet the need to be with students of the opposite sex.

Sharing with other class groups what has been learned also serves as a reinforcement and affirmation for the learning gained. Moreover, the sharing time will provide motivation to complete the learning assignments (Bible learning methods) in the class groups, and will help to increase learners' self-esteem as they begin to sense that their sharing God's truths with the other groups is a form of ministry for them.

Sometimes the classes will do things together as a large group—like brainstorming lists, watching films, listening to speakers, discussing questions, etc. Sometimes learners will work with only their class group to do an assignment. Then the two groups will share with each other what they did. Let us look at what a lesson in this department might involve.

Students begin in the large group by brainstorming together what they think of when they think of prayer. Then each class group is given a Bible Exploration project. The boys study James 1:1-5 about praying for wisdom and the girls study some of Christ's promises to answer prayer. After about 15 minutes, the groups share with each other what they have learned. Then for Life Exploration each group is given a different case study to discuss and some questions to answer. After discussing in their class groups for 10 minutes, the groups again tell each other what they learned. For the Conclusion-Decision the students share with their group one area of their life where they need prayer and close by praying for each other. (See chapter 5, Planning the Session Methods for further discussion of planning a session.)

If classes work together in a department there needs to be one teacher for each of the class groups. These teachers plan together what will happen during the Bible study session. In addition, one person needs to be responsible for coordinating the session time, giving any instructions which need to be given to the entire department, guiding the times when class groups share what they have learned, and the 1001 other details that always seem to crop up when people work together. It is easiest if this person, called a department leader, is not one of the teachers since there are so many things to do.

It is also helpful if each department has a secretary to keep track of attendance, visitors, and supplies. Chapter 7 talks further about the jobs of the different department workers.

How Do We Group Classes into Departments?

Remember the department has one or more classes working together on the same materials.

Even the smallest youth program should have two departments: junior high and senior high school.

Here are several ways you might group classes together to form departments:

FIGURE 2

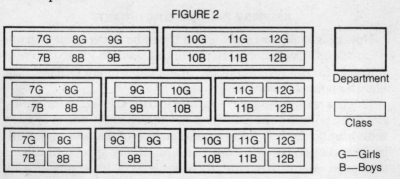

| 7G | 8G | 9G |
| 7B | 8B | 9B |

| 10G | 11G | 12G |
| 10B | 11B | 12B |

Department

| 7G | 8G |
| 7B | 8B |

| 9G | 10G |
| 9B | 10B |

| 11G | 12G |
| 11B | 12B |

Class

| 7G | 8G |
| 7B | 8B |

| 9G | 9G |
| 9B |

| 10G | 11G | 12G |
| 10B | 11B | 12B |

G—Girls
B—Boys

Be aware that if a department has more than five classes, it becomes cumbersome to coordinate, sharing of projects takes up too much time, and effective learning becomes more difficult. It is then time to think of forming two departments.

Keep in mind that 8 learners is a sufficient number to create a department (8 will be enough for 2 classes or small groups), and that 40 learners (5 groups of 8 learners each) ought to be considered a maximum for maintaining good teaching practices within a department.

When choosing a plan to use in grouping learners into departments for youth teaching, there are two other factors which ought to be considered.

a. Large numbers in a department tend to promote feelings of success, unity and group identity.

b. If the age span is too wide, needs may not be adequately met (ninth graders and twelfth graders do not have much in common).

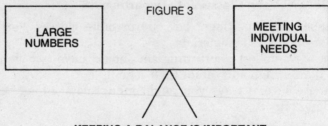

FIGURE 3

LARGE NUMBERS

MEETING INDIVIDUAL NEEDS

KEEPING A BALANCE IS IMPORTANT

How do you choose curriculum if you have two grades in one department? Cycle the curriculum. Use seventh grade materials this year for the seventh-eighth grade department and then use eighth grade curriculum next year.

There is no one right way to group learners. Effective grouping involves tailoring the plan to meet the specific needs of each individual church. It takes careful survey of the present enrollment and attendance, a consideration of any special problems that exist within the church, as well as a little imaginative guesstimating about the natural growth possibilities to devise a workable pattern.

Remember to choose a grouping pattern only after considering several possibilities and to anticipate changing the grouping pattern. Adapting to growth is the key to effective grouping.

WHAT DO WE DO WHEN WE GROW?

You grouped your students into class groups of three to eight each. With five it is easy to get everyone involved. But when you grow to 10 learners in a group, the shy members can get by with just listening, not everyone gets a chance to share, and other problems develop.

FIGURE 4 ■ **Possible interactions and interpersonal relationships in a group**

What do you do?

Create a New Class Group

Creating a new class group can be a simple and nonthreatening process when careful preplanning is done.

Step One: When a class group grows large enough to create two groups, have a new teacher sit in the group with the regular teacher to observe and become acquainted with the young people.

Step Two: Plan two Bible learning methods for the group and invite the learners to subdivide to complete both assignments. The new teacher directs one team and the original teacher the

FIGURE 5 ■ **CREATING A NEW SMALL GROUP**

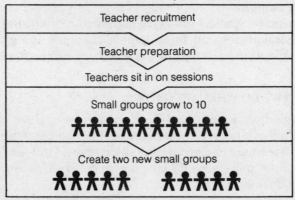

other. Let the learners choose which assignment they wish to work on (as long as the two groups are more or less equal in the number of learners). Some learners will group themselves by their friendships. This is fine, unless the friendship begins to interfere with the learning process.

Be sure to keep both teams (small groups) in the same room. This is absolutely critical! If we go to separate rooms, we have been divided, "And I don't want to be divided from my friends!" But if we stay in the same room, we are creating new units: "Isn't it neat how we are growing?"

Step Three: Repeat the process of planning two Bible learning methods and of allowing learners to continue to choose their subgroup for three to four weeks. Then begin to firm up the membership of the two new class groups. Keeping the same people in the same class groups over a period of time is important because of the relationships built within the group. The deeper the relationships, the more open and honest will be the sharing of personal problems and growth.

Create a New Department

When your classes grow and form new classes, you will eventually grow to where you have more than five groups in a department. Coordination of teachers and learners grows difficult, sharing what all the learners have discovered begins to take so long that learning is impaired, and it is time to form a new department. This can also be a simple procedure if planned carefully.

Step One: Plan for and recruit additional staff as necessary.

Step Two: Locate a suitable place to meet.

Step Three: If you have been a two-grade department (i.e., ninth and tenth grades), making a separation by grade may be the easiest choice. If not, choose the grouping pattern which seems most logical and most probable to succeed.

Remember not to segregate departments by sex...but rather have small groups of guys and small groups of girls in both departments. The guys need to hear God revealing truth and insights through the girls, and the girls need to hear God revealing truth and spiritual insights through the guys. It will increase their spiritual appreciation of each other.

Step Four: Move the small groups as units with their teachers, rather than breaking up small groups and/or bringing in new teachers.

READY TO GO?

Sometimes it is difficult for us as teachers to set aside the traditional patterns for the use of time, facilities and grouping learners within the Bible study session, in exchange for concepts that seem new to us. Often the difficulty lies in that the old ways are familiar and we feel at least somewhat comfortable with them.

But as you reconsider your objectives in teaching and reevaluate these suggestions for facilitating learning, we trust that you will be excited as you consider new and effective ways to organize for learning for your youth.

Organizing Your Teaching Time

"I know, I know!" Gene began excitedly, bouncing up and down in his eagerness to contribute to the discussion.

Just then the buzzer rang, and time was up. Don groaned silently, sharing the disappointment of the learners in his tenth grade Bible study session.

"Every time we get started on something that's really interesting," one of the boys complained, "that buzzer stops everything! We never have enough time!"

Even as he promised to continue the discussion on the following week, Don knew the boy was right. Time was a real problem. Every minute in the small group was precious, and spending even a few minutes next week finishing this discussion would take away time from the session for that morning. Furthermore, Gene's moment of discovery would be hard to recapture.

Don thought back over his planning. What could he do differently? He chose his content prayerfully. He planned for the learners to be involved by keeping his lecture time to a minimum. But after the departmental opening exercises there were only 29 minutes left for Bible study time. And every week, just when the group would really get rolling, time was up.

Don heard very little of the pastor's sermon that morning as he puzzled over his problem. Later, after a quiet lunch, while he sat drinking his coffee, his wife Betty probed gently, "Ready to talk about it?"

"I get really frustrated every week," Don began. "It's the same old story. We don't have enough time to get through the Bible information, let alone to drawing any meaningful conclusions. There must be a practical solution!"

Betty smiled. "Well, what all are you trying to do during the session?"

"We get started with a couple of warm-up songs, some announcements, the offering, a devotional—sort of a spiritual life challenge, prayer and end up with about 29 minutes for Bible study. I guess we really try to accomplish three basic things: worship, announcements, and Bible study. The announcements don't usually take up too much time, but how can we have a meaningful worship time and a good Bible study in just under an hour a week? I just don't know *what* to do!" He finished with a shrug.

THE GOAL AND THE PROBLEM

Many teachers find themselves struggling with the same frustrations that Don faces. They sincerely desire to teach the Bible in the most effective way possible. That means they must get students actively involved in the learning process. But actively involving students in the learning process takes more time. Thus the teacher is faced with two basic problems:

1) How much and which content does he cover?

2) How does he plan for effective participation learning?

Let us take a look at how to select content for teaching; the essential elements of a good lesson; how to use time more effectively through unit teaching and total session teaching; and how to adapt lesson plans for your time period.

SELECTING CONTENT

Have you ever looked at the lesson in your curriculum manual or at a Bible passage and thought with exasperation, "I can't cover all that! I only have...minutes!"

Choose a Focus

The first thing to consider when planning a session is selecting a focus. Ask yourself: "What one fact or concept from this Scripture passage do my learners need most to grasp?" There may be several possible focuses. Select the one that is best for your learners. As you make that idea, fact or concept the center of your teaching for the hour, all other facts and ideas from that passage will be examined as they relate to the focus.

To illustrate how a focus helps in planning, think of a pebble thrown into a pond and sending forth ripples. You concentrate the learning on the center and only include as much of the supporting information as the time allows. More learning will occur if you concentrate well on one idea rather than if you try to touch on every concept in the passage.

FIGURE 1

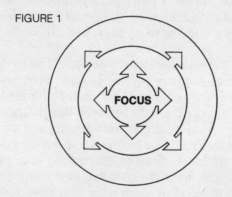

FOCUS

Consider Learners' Needs

Next ask yourself, "How does this focus relate to my learners' needs?" For example, assume your focus is "praying for specific needs." Perhaps Sally needs to pray about her problem relating to her parents and Joe needs to pray about asking forgiveness from Tom. Eddie told one of the counselors he prayed about a test, but he still flunked it. Therefore he was not going to trust God to answer a prayer again. Keeping that in mind you know that part of your session needs to help students understand what kinds of things to pray for and how to handle the answers they get.

If a teacher wants to see lives changed as a result of exciting Bible study, the material studied must relate to specific student needs.

Formulate Objectives

After you have identified the focus and you have considered what your students' needs are, then select objectives (aims, goals) which are appropriate for the focus and the individual learners in your group. Objectives (goals, aims) simply answer the question, "What will my students do or be able to do as a result of studying this session?" These objectives may involve Bible information students will identify; applications, concepts or ideas students will discuss; or specific responses and life changes students will make as they put the Bible principles into practice.

"But why do I need objectives?" you ask. The basic reason is that if you aim at nothing that is usually what you will hit. Objectives give the teacher a direction for planning a session which will encourage learners to make life changes. It is like planning a trip. You do not just start driving and say, "I hope I end up somewhere nice." You look at a map, select a destination, and then plan the most effective, interesting way to get there. Effective teaching is the same way. You select a destination you would like your learners to reach with you. Then you plan how to get there.

What makes a good objective? There are at least three ways to evaluate an objective.

Is it ownable? An objective is ownable if you believe the learner would like to have this objective reached in his life, or should be at least willing to try it. Objectives that are not ownable result in reluctant learners and will usually not produce significant change within the learner.

Is it reachable? is the second test of a good objective. An objective is reachable if it is reasonable to assume that your learner can accomplish it. Unreachable objectives reinforce failure and deny, in the learner's mind, that Christ's strength is adequate for his every need. If a learner continually experiences failure and frustration in trying to reach your learning goals, he will eventually see himself as incapable of learning and also begin doing things to avoid the "negative" experiences.

Is it measurable? is the third test of a good objective. An objective is measurable if you have some observable method of being able to tell when the learner has accomplished it. Both the learner and the teacher must be able to tell when the objective has been met.

Let us examine some objectives using these three standards for measurement. Read each of the following objectives. For each one, if it is ownable circle the **O**, if it is reachable the **R**, and if it is measurable the **M**.

O   R   M As a result of this session my learners should lead a friend to Christ.

O   R   M By the end of this session my learners should understand the importance of prayer.

The first objective is ownable, if you can believe that the learners should be willing to try to lead a friend to Christ. Thus this objective would not be ownable for students who are not Christians. The objective is easily measurable. You will be able to talk to any student who becomes a Christian. However, this objective is not reachable for all of your learners because leading a friend to Christ requires cooperation that is beyond the control of the learners.

A better objective would be: "After this session my learners will tell one person about Christ's love for him." It is reasonable to assume that every learner could tell someone else.

The second objective is both ownable and reachable, but it is extremely difficult to measure "understanding." A better way to write this objective would be: "By the end of this session, my learners will explain three reasons prayer is important for Christians."

In the classroom good objectives are a real help. They assist the teacher to design a session which encourages specific change in learners' lives. These objectives help the teacher focus the direction of the teaching within the session time and provide guidelines for measuring the spiritual growth of the learners.

Good objectives 1) guide learners' work toward specific spiritual goals; 2) help learners translate spiritual understanding into workable plans which make them doers of the Word; 3) help learners feel a sense of responsibility and accountability to other Christians as they share how they are doing; and 4) provide guidelines for measuring spiritual growth in their own lives.

Remember how the Israelites built altars in honor of special encounters with God, and how those altars became monuments to God at work in their lives? In the same way, objectives reached in the lives of your learners can become monuments to God at work in their lives!

To assist learners in successfully building monuments to spiritual growth, you will use long-range and short-range objectives. The more precisely you can define your learning objectives, the more likely you are to do the right thing to achieve those results.

In order to assist the learner in making a major change in his life, the teacher needs to plan several sub-objectives. First, the learner will discover what God has to say about the desired behavior. Next, the learner will discuss how his attitude and current behavior might need to change in light of what he has discovered. He will need to look at the new life-style, discuss the implications and results, examine practical applications. Finally, the learner will make specific plans to assume the responsibility for practicing and actually adopting the new behavior.

Remember, change takes time, and it is an orderly process.

Difficult or complicated objectives can be reached if they are divided into several small, achievable steps as sub-objectives. For example, assume your goal is that students will pray once a day. You may need to have sub-objectives that students will be able to explain three biblical illustrations of answered prayer; to list five verses where God promises to answer prayer; to list and discuss five benefits of prayer; etc.

"But I don't have that much time!" you cry. Then consider teaching in units.

UNIT TEACHING

It takes time to guide learners to make specific life changes as a result of their study of Scripture. One week may not be long enough. Did you become a Christian the very first time you heard the gospel? Did you consecrate your life the first time you heard the challenge? Probably not. Is it reasonable, therefore, to expect learners to make major life changes the first time they hear what is expected of them? Probably not!

For this reason, a teacher may plan several weeks of study with a single focus or objective. A series of sessions which relate to the same focus or objectives is called a unit. Remember the objective for teaching students about prayer which we divided into several sub-objectives? In a unit on prayer, each session of the unit would have its own sub-objective which would serve as one of the essential steps in reaching the unit objective.

There are several benefits of teaching in units. Having several sessions related to the same focus provides a sense of continuity for learners. It is easier to plan several sessions which are related rather than a totally new topic each week. It is easier to follow up on projects students initiate in their lives. Furthermore, a learner has several chances to consider change in his attitudes and actions. Thus you will note a larger number of students making commitments to change.

PLANNING THE SESSION

Once you have chosen a focus from the Scripture, and have set good learner objectives (for the unit and the sessions), your next task is to plan ways to involve the learners actively in the learning process during the Bible study session.

An effective youth Bible study has four parts:

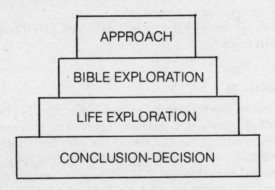

APPROACH

BIBLE EXPLORATION

LIFE EXPLORATION

CONCLUSION-DECISION

Each part of the session has a specific purpose and a logical place in the learning sequence.

The Approach

When learners arrive, often their thoughts are still on last night's party, the last conversation, this morning's argument at home before coming. The *Approach* focuses the learners' interest on the topic or theme of the Bible study for the day.

Because the *Approach* focuses the learners' attention on the topic of the Bible study session, you will want to use a method which will do just that as quickly as possible. The *Approach* is usually the shortest part of the session (2 to 10 minutes) and does not normally include debates, long reports, research or problem solving assignments.

The *Approach* method may involve learners individually, in small groups, or all together in a large group. For example, if you are going to study prayer you might have individuals answer two or three questions about their own prayer life on a questionnaire; or have students share in threes about an answered prayer they or a friend experienced; or as a large group brainstorm things teenagers pray about most. The goal is to get learners thinking about your topic and to do it as quickly and effectively as possible.

When their interest has been captured, learners are then ready to begin *Bible Exploration*.

Bible Exploration

The successful teacher helps his learners systematically discover God's principles and truths from the Bible. If Christian young people are ever to have "the mind of Christ" they must be consistently and continually learning from, and grounded, in God's Word.

The *Bible Exploration* is when learners explore and discover God's point of view in the Scriptures. Before learners can apply God's principles to everyday life situations, they must *thoroughly* understand those principles. How can someone explain how to handle temptation the way God would want him to, unless he knows what God has to say about handling temptation? Therefore a well-planned *Bible Exploration* directly involves learners in analyzing, researching, discussing and understanding the Scriptures.

Bible Exploration methods may involve learners individually, in small groups, or all together in a large group. You may want to have students list several points in a passage; identify and describe main characters, events or principles; paraphrase passages; illustrate narratives; etc. Whatever methods you choose, they should force the students to examine the Scripture passage carefully, identify the main points, and help them come to a more thorough understanding of those ideas.

Often this is most effectively done when students work together in small groups of two to eight. In small groups learners have more opportunity to interact with each other and with the teacher, learners needing more guidance can receive help, and enthusiasm is shared which makes learning more fun.

Having each small group report to other groups what they studied is one way for your learners to share what they have learned during the *Bible Exploration*. This gives an excellent opportunity for them to demonstrate that they understand what God has to say, and a chance for you to correct misunderstandings.

What happens when they do not share all that you had in mind for them to discover? Ask yourself if it is absolutely necessary to know the omitted points. If so and if time permits, use questions to lead them to discover the missing information. You can also affirm the learners for what God is teaching them and then share what God has been teaching you from that passage. However, use this second technique sparingly so that learners do not begin to feel the teacher will always "top" what they are learning.

Mutual sharing—the learners first and then teacher affirming and adding other insights or information—can be exciting when you establish the atmosphere that you are learners together of God's Word. And, you will be surprised how interested they are in what you have to say when they realize you are listening to them too.

Life Exploration

When learners clearly understand the Bible principles studied, they are ready to begin *Life Exploration*. During *Life Exploration* the learners examine possibilities for applying the biblical principles discovered during *Bible Exploration* to contemporary living.

Life Exploration provides opportunities for learners to discuss, research, demonstrate and practice applying God's principles to today's world. Endeavoring to apply God's principles to contemporary situations should prove to be stimulating to learners, and many nitty-gritty discussions about basic Christian living should be a natural result. However this is a learning step unfortunately omitted by many teachers.

It is essential that students have an opportunity to discuss how to apply God's principles to contemporary situations *before* considering what to do in their own lives. As students discuss what a young person could/should do in applying the Bible principles, they often hear new ideas about what they could do in their own lives; misconceptions are exposed and corrected; learners evaluate the benefits, costs and implications of change; and learners form a better basis for evaluating their own readiness personally to apply God's principles.

Teachers will get clues about where individual learners are in the learning process from their participation at this point. Is Janet excitedly volunteering answers? She may just have discovered how God's principles can help with a special situation. Is Sharon, who had no problem identifying principles during *Bible Exploration*, unable or unwilling to participate? She may be having difficulty seeing the relationship between the scriptural facts and the contemporary situation. Or, she may be resisting the Holy Spirit's guidance in this aspect.

Bible learning methods for this part of the session may involve learners individually or all together in a large group, *but small groups usually provide the best setting for Life Exploration*. Small group interaction allows students to struggle together to think of ideas. It provides a chance for immediate feedback and discussion. Students have the encouragement of knowing what their peers are thinking. Also, most students will more readily share ideas in the small group than in a large group.

Because students are talking about specific problems, many teachers find a deeper level of sharing and honesty when guys are together in groups and gals are together at this stage. (It is difficult for a guy who is trying to impress the gal sitting across from him to talk about the fears and failures young men struggle with.) Deeper sharing will also more readily develop if students are in the same group several weeks so trust can grow.

If sharing what has been accomplished during this time would be helpful and reinforcing for the other small groups, you will want to plan time for sharing in the large group again.

When learners have successfully demonstrated that they understand how to apply the session truths to contemporary realities, they are ready to personalize their learning experience. They are ready for *Conclusion-Decision*.

Conclusion-Decision

The *Conclusion-Decision* part of the session is the time when the learner is given an opportunity to decide how he will use the Bible information in his own everyday life. Some learners will appropriate God's principles at this point and make specific plans for specific situations they are facing. This is *not* the time for sweeping generalities typical of the New Year's resolution: "I'll never yield to temptation again!" This *is* a time for very specific and reachable plans: "I will not cheat on Thursday's exam."

Bible learning methods for this part of the session may involve learners individually, in small groups, or all together as a large group. However, learners will feel more free to share personal applications, problems and experiences if they are in a supportive small group. Again that means guys together, girls together, and groups where trust has been developed over a period of several sessions spent together.

Did you narrow the focus of study and write ownable, reachable and measurable objectives for your learners when you planned the session? Did the learning methods support the focus and objectives? Then the plans your learners write should be consistent with the objectives you wrote for them. However, remember that it is the Holy Spirit who changes lives and we must wait for His timing. Some students may not be ready to commit themselves to applying God's principles. Do not try to force, coerce, shame, embarrass or manipulate them into change. Instead love them, accept them as they are, and pray for them.

FIGURE 2 ■ **SESSION PLAN SHEET**

Unit title _____	Title _____ Date _____
Unit focus _____	Scripture _____
_____	Focus _____
Unit aims _____	Aims _____
_____	_____
_____	_____

TIME	Bible Learning Activites **APPROACH**	Teacher Resp.	Supplies Needed
	BIBLE EXPLORATION (indicate each group's assignment)		
	LIFE EXPLORATION (indicate each group's assignment)		
	CONCLUSION-DECISION		

Follow-up

You can reinforce learners who act on their plans to make life changes based on God's Word, by following up with them. This gives them an opportunity to share victories with those who care. You can encourage learners who did not carry out their plans to make new commitments to try again. You can help learners who tried and failed to try again. They may need additional input, a change in the plan or just another chance. To be encouraged by someone who believes in them may be just what they need to become winners.

Accountability is still the key to responsibility. If your learners know that you will follow up on their plans and that you really care about their lives, they will take their decisions more seriously.

You can follow up with a phone call, "How was the exam?" a postcard, or a personal visit. Perhaps you will follow up by having a sharing time during the next week's session.

Keep your follow-up encouraging. Do not give the impression that you are checking up on your learners, because you did not trust them or just to fulfill a responsibility. Instead show loving concern for their personal growth and exciting expectations to see God's power at work in their lives.

When your follow-up verifies that the learners are truly applying God's principles in their lives as a result of what they explored and discovered in the Bible study session, you can be sure that learning has occurred!

SOME LAST THOUGHTS ON CHOOSING METHODS

Designing a lesson plan should begin with: 1) What do I want the learners to accomplish during the session? 2) What learning methods will best help them accomplish that? Part 4 of this book gives ideas on selecting specific methods. As you plan and select methods keep in mind that a department with two to five class groups can work together as a large group, break into class groups, or even break into smaller groups of twos or threes. One class group that meets by itself can also meet as a large group (the entire class), work as smaller groups (a class of eight can break into two groups of four each), or even break into teams of twos to work also. Furthermore, keep in mind that any one of the four parts of the session (Approach, Bible Exploration, Life Exploration, Conclusion-Decision) can be designed to use either large or small group methods.

As you plan also remember that methods are not an end in themselves. They are ways that you help the students come into direct contact with God's Word, examine what God has to say and try applying it to their own lives. Sometimes discussions get off the track and many different ideas are mentioned. Therefore, it is often helpful at the end of an activity or sharing time to summarize the main points in one or two sentences.

Finally, evaluate your lessons after you teach.

■ Did the students come up with the main points?
■ Were there points of confusion? If so, why?
■ How much did you talk and how much did the students talk? Was there anyone who didn't talk at all?
■ Were your instructions clear?
■ Were the methods good ones for your students?
■ What new thing did you learn about each of your students and what God is teaching him or her?
■ How could you do better next time?

WHAT ABOUT TIME?

Another factor that may influence your choice of methods will be the time available for the session. It would be an obvious understatement to say that you can be more creative in 60 minutes than in 30 minutes. Creative learning that involves the learners actively in the learning process does increase the time required, but it also increases the retention and the transference of ownership of biblical truths on the part of the learners. Creative involvement at each phase of the session plan does require time, especially if you have several groups who will need to share what they have discovered.

FIGURE 3

5–10 minutes	**APPROACH**
15–25 minutes	**BIBLE EXPLORATION** Preparation (Creative Method) Reporting and Sharing
15–25 minutes	**LIFE EXPLORATION** Preparation (Creative Method) Reporting and Sharing
5–10 minutes	**CONCLUSION-DECISION**

If you have less than an hour available for your teaching time, you will need to make some important decisions about how you will allot the time during the teaching session. If you have several classes working together as a department, one way to conserve time is to complete both the Bible and Life Exploration assignments before sharing and reporting in the large group.

FIGURE 4

5–10 minutes	**APPROACH**
20–40 minutes	**BIBLE EXPLORATION** and **LIFE EXPLORATION** Preparation
5–10 minutes	Reporting and Sharing
5–10 minutes	**CONCLUSION-DECISION**

Another way to conserve time is to have a creative or more time-consuming Bible Exploration method, but a simple or relatively quick Life Exploration method.

FIGURE 5

5 minutes	**APPROACH**
15 minutes	**BIBLE EXPLORATION** (Creative Method)
5 minutes	**LIFE EXPLORATION** (Short discussion. Sharing of ideas)
5 minutes	**CONCLUSION-DECISION**

Or you might have a short Bible Exploration method and a longer, more involved Life Exploration method.

FIGURE 6

5 minutes	**APPROACH**
5 minutes	**BIBLE EXPLORATION** (Listing of facts and principles)
15 minutes	**LIFE EXPLORATION** (Creative Method)
5 minutes	**CONCLUSION-DECISION**

There may even be sessions where you want students to stay together the entire time in the large group for a special presentation or a film. There may be times when students will come into class, go straight to their small groups, and never come together to share. The key is: What are your learning objectives? What methods are appropriate?

Consider Total Session Teaching

Many churches divide their allotted Bible study session time between opening exercises (also called department time, assembly time, worship time, opening assembly, or closing assembly) and class time. The number of students and the layout of the facilities generally determine if everyone meets together for opening exercises or if children, youth and adults meet separately.

Singing, announcements, offering, special music, introduction of visitors, birthday wishes, testimonies, a devotional by one of the teachers, and taking attendance are some of the planned activities for opening exercises. Some of the unplanned activities include whispering, giggling, note passing and a little friendly shoving among the younger, more restless boys.

However well prepared the leaders are, most learners seem to treat the opening exercises as if they were just something one does while waiting to go to class. Most churches lose from 15–30 valuable minutes every week because many young people have tuned out opening exercises. Furthermore, although most of the small group or class time is spent in teaching, those 25–30 minutes just are not enough to allow learners to become really involved in the learning process. *Time is a limiting factor!*

One solution to time shortage is to reevaluate the total church program and see if somehow you can get more time for the teaching program.

Another solution to this time shortage is *Total Session Teaching*. This means that:

a. The entire session time is given to teaching and setting the stage for learning.
b. All of the learning methods, activities and songs for each session relate to one subject.

If you have an opening session with a variety of students from a variety of classes studying a variety of different topics, it will be difficult to have the songs, etc., relate to the subject each class is studying. Because of this and because of a sincere desire to do the best possible job teaching God's Word to young people, many teachers choose to omit the large group opening sessions. Singspirations are often more meaningful on a Sunday evening or during the week. Music is also a great learning activity; use it as such when it fits. Introduction of visitors may be more practical in classes or small groups, where getting involved is easier than during the large group opening. Prayer may be more meaningful if it is an integral part of the session, and the offering could be taken on the way into the session. Announcements can be placed on bulletin boards or mimeographed as pass-outs.

Organizing Your Facilities

Happy sounds of youthful spirits high on the promise of adventure drew the attention of even the most seasoned sea veteran. Clad in bold-colored pullovers, faded Levis and brand-new sneakers, a group of Christian young people clambered aboard the docked sailboat. Although it was the first trip for this particular group, the week-long sail from Los Angeles to Catalina Island and back had become an annual event for the boat and its owner.

Several weeks before the sail, each young person had received a list of things to bring and a labeled diagram of the sailboat with instructions to learn "the lingo."

Cries of "Look off starboard!" and "He just went aft looking for you, dumbo!" reflected the hours of homework that had been spent in memorizing the unfamiliar terms. However, the young people were not sailors yet! If the boat had been turned over to them even while it was still in the harbor, there would have been trouble. Big trouble!

But only one week later the captain smiled contentedly as he relinquished control to the group—now a crew. They sailed in through the harbor by themselves, gently nosing the boat into the slip. All went well.

In a week's time, in the right environment, these landlubbers had become sailors. Why?

While the new environment itself did not effect the change, it did play a vital role. Suddenly the memorized words and that diagram were visualized as three-dimensional realities. Only by taking an active part in directing the boat's functions and putting theories into practice did the young people experience a learning phenomenon... *They changed.*

THE CHALLENGE

Everyday life situations are also the best environment for teaching God's truths. Much of Jesus' teaching was on-the-spot in the natural environment of His learners. His teaching situations included the Sea of Galilee, fishing boats, shepherds with their flocks, wells for drawing water, a marriage feast, the synagogue, sorrow over sickness, a funeral, a storm, and a fig tree. Jesus used creatively the situations that the people confronted daily. He sat on a mountain and looked over the multitudes. "Consider the lilies of the field," He urged as He taught them faith. "Believe when you pray!" He taught as He cursed the fig tree and it withered away.

In the Old Testament Moses encouraged the Israelites to teach God's truth to their children in their own homes where they worked, played, rested and laughed. Learning was achieved in the environment of family relationships and experience.

Yet, how do we do it? We teach skiing on the slopes, swimming in the water and cooking in the kitchen. But we attempt to teach life values and Christian behavior in a classroom.

Our learners do not live in the classroom. They live in a real world made up of relationships, conflicts, temptations, opportunities, constraints, and choices. So how does the Bible teacher make a classroom with four walls an exciting place to learn about God and His Word? The environment you instruct in can be either an asset or a liability. It all depends on how you use the facilities. You must *create* a stimulating learning environment —it will not just happen by itself. It is a real challenge, but it is worth the effort in order to develop a learning environment which supports and enriches your teaching.

The teacher, learners and learning methods are the most important part of the learning environment. The most perfect of rooms with a poor teacher or poor methods will not be stimulating. However, effective use of your facilities can be a dynamic asset. Let us examine some ways in which facilities can be used to create a more effective learning environment.

LET'S LOOK AT THE ROOM

Most churches have constructed traditional facilities that have small classrooms leading off from a large assembly room.

This provides for small group instruction as well as large group worship and other activities. This arrangement is especially suitable to a youth division that is organized on a class level where each class meets alone. If your youth division is organized this way, you will still need to follow the guidelines in chapter 5 for planning. You may also want to meet together

FIGURE 1 ■ **ASSEMBLY/CLASSROOM ARRANGEMENT**

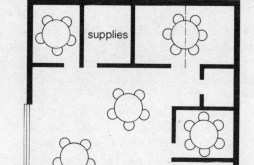

with another class in the assembly room at the end of some sessions or units and have students share some of the things they have learned.

Youth divisions organized on a department level (several classes working together) often prefer an open room design for their facilities. Instead of meeting in small adjoining classrooms, all of the small groups in a department meet in one large assembly room. The groups of learners work in various parts of the room, and a teacher in each group leads the activities.

The ideal room for department teaching is a well-equipped room of approximately 900 square feet (30'x30' or 10x10 m). This is large enough to accommodate a large group of 30 comfortably, but when necessary can accommodate up to 40 youth. In a room this size, the department members can work in small class groups and still remain in the same room.

The value of being able to remain in one room is most important because of time and continuity for the session. If learners do

FIGURE 2 ■ **OPEN ROOM ENVIRONMENT**

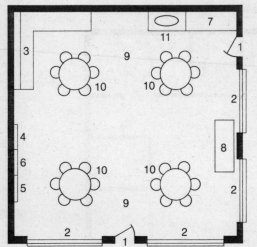

1. Door
2. Window
3. Book and
   magazine rack
4. Tack board
5. Chalkboard
6. Screen
7. Supply closet
8. Table
9. Possible
   department center
10. Chairs
11. Sink

not have to travel when the activity changes from large group to small, they can begin working immediately on their tasks. This saves at least five learning minutes per change.

Another important value of remaining in one room is that the department leader can plan to vary the sessions more. The small groups can work separately or together as a department without any complicated instructions about which room to go to and when to return, etc. Instead, a change becomes simply a matter of changing the center of attention from within the small circle of chairs, to the center of the room for a large group activity and back again for a small group activity. The number of changes possible in this way is virtually endless.

On the surface this kind of environment might seem to have one obvious disadvantage: During small group time, more than one person in the room is talking. However, this is less of a problem than many teachers imagine it to be. Think of how people manage to communicate efficiently to a whole table of friends at a restaurant without bothering the adjacent tables. Or notice how people will center their attention on conversation in the small group of people in which they are, rather than on everyone else in a crowded lobby.

If a learner is involved in the activities of his small group, he will direct his attention to his group even though another small group is working right next to his. However, sometimes learners will be so interested in their groups that you may even find yourself saying to a noisy group, "It is really exciting to see how enthusiastic you are about your assignment, but the next group is having trouble concentrating. Hold it down a little, OK?"

If your eductional building is constructed on the assembly/ class design and you would like to implement department teaching, you can adapt your facility. Remove the doors from the small classrooms or allow them to stand open during the teaching session. In addition to assigning class groups to the small classrooms, place two or more activities in the adjoining assembly area at the same time.

BE PROPERLY EQUIPPED

There are some general requirements for all classrooms, regardless of size or design. Classrooms should have proper lighting, heating, cooling and ventilation. Good acoustics are also an asset. The walls of the classroom should be soundproof, the ceiling acoustically treated, and the floor carpeted if possible. There should be electrical outlets located conveniently throughout the room for tape recorders and slide, filmstrip, motion picture, overhead, or opaque projectors.

Be sure that your room contains sufficient chairs and work tables (when needed for specific learning methods) of appropriate size, cabinets or closets for storage, a permanent or portable chalkboard and a bulletin board for displaying visual aids. A portable projection screen should be available if a permanent one has not been installed.

You will want to provide extra Bibles and study helps which will make Bible study easier and quicker—concordance, Bible dictionary, dictionary of the English language, Bible handbook, several versions of Scripture, a bibliography of Bible exposition, world atlas, Bible atlas and maybe a set of commentaries. If you cannot purchase these supplies for your youth department, then try to give your learners access to these resources through your church or personal library. Teach youth how to find answers on their own and how to use Bible study helps.

Audiovisual equipment is important to have available—film and slide projectors, cassette recorders, record players, etc. You can greatly increase the effectiveness of your teaching through the use of audiovisuals (see chapter 11). Films and filmstrips are available from local library and church film supplier. Records, cassettes, pre-recorded dramas and interviews, slides, and multi-media presentations can all be effective.

A PICTURE IS WORTH A THOUSAND WORDS

Even if your class must meet in a broom closet, a few colorful posters can do wonders to create a more cheerful, inviting learning environment. Those posters should include projects students make as a part of their Bible learning.

Does your room need to be painted? If possible, let the students do it. This will help them feel the room is really "theirs" and build a sense of community as they work together to better their room.

BRING THE REAL WORLD TO CLASS

Another way to bring the real world into the classroom is to bring in physical objects appropriate to the study. When teaching about the vine in John 15, bring in a potted plant. If the real thing is not available, models, or pictures can be valuable. Filmstrips, motion pictures or videotapes can bring the outside world into the room. Even chalkboard sketches can be used to illustrate unfamiliar objects.

One teacher, while studying Gideon and the tearing down of the altar of Baal, asked his senior high boys each to bring a teenage idol the next week. They did. They brought:

a deck of cards—to show worship of leisure time activities

a music book—to show worship of pop music which imposes wrong ideas

a basketball—to show worship of sports

a dollar bill—to show worship of money

wine bottle (empty)—to show worship of worldly pleasures.

What was interesting to note was that as they shared it was apparent that each had brought the one "idol" he was most tempted to bow to.

That was a session the guys still talk about. They gained new insights and appreciations for each other that day. They ended the session in a time of prayer for each other. A really powerful time!

Having learners reenact biblical events is another way to simulate real life in the classroom. Spontaneous drama, skits, demonstrations or roleplays can help learners feel the emotions and face the choices they would have in similar experiences. These "experiences" also give the learners an opportunity to practice responses to difficult situations without suffering real life consequences.

VARY THE ROOM ARRANGEMENT

Let the session plan dictate the arrangement of your classroom. Is a large group presentation planned? Arrange the chairs in a semicircle (rather than in neat, tight, rows). Are both large and small group assignments planned? Arrange the chairs in small groups before students arrive. Are Bible learning methods planned which will require learners to work at tables? Provide enough tables with appropriate supplies to accommodate those groups that will need them. (If the groups will not need the tables for the entire session, and if there is room, you may wish to place the tables around the sides of the room.)

To table or not to table, that is the question. Some say that a table separates people psychologically; others say "nonsense." And again we hear, "A good place to lay your Bible." "But, it's hard to hear. A circle's the thing." You have to decide. You might consider a circle for the Bible search and discussion, and moving to a table for projects. At any rate, preserving the intimate atmosphere of the small group is of greater importance than "table" or "circle."

ONE LAST PROBLEM

The biggest problem with developing creative environments for teaching is the often-heard cry, "But we can't afford that kind of building...or room...or equipment!" You may not be able to equip your facility perfectly overnight, but you must set your priorities and begin somewhere. Select some of the things which you can do right now. Work in both short-range and long-range plans for change. Obtain the needed equipment gradually. Remodel or adapt a building over a period of time. Purchase items or suggest them as gifts one at a time. As you set priorities, you are planning for the upgrading of the learning environment. And as you upgrade the learning environment, you should begin to see learners motivated to greater learning and retention.

PART 3

HELP YOUR LEADERS GROW

A LOOK AT THE LEADERS

FINDING AND TRAINING LEADERS

WORKING TOGETHER

A Look at the Leaders

"I'll miss you, Dottie," whispered Beth tearfully after class as she gave her teacher an affectionate hug and hurried out of the classroom to join the other girls.

"I'll miss you, too," Dottie replied aloud, her words echoing in the empty room. "I'll miss every one of the girls."

It was Dottie's last Sunday to teach her ninth grade class. She had accepted a job promotion in another city and next week she was moving away. Reluctant to leave the classroom just yet, Dottie wandered around the room straightening the chairs, gathering up pencils, and erasing the chalkboard. As she stopped and stared unseeingly out the window, she reviewed her last four years as a Bible teacher. "I've really learned a lot in these years," she thought, smiling at the memory of the early days.

When first approached about teaching a class, Dottie thought that teaching meant reading a printed lesson from a teacher's manual on Saturday night and paraphrasing the material on Sunday morning. She was willing, but not too excited. Now, she was considered one of the most dynamic, well-liked and effective teachers in the church. She had learned her role well, and had enhanced her teaching talents by developing the required characteristics.

Every leader in your youth teaching ministry should follow Dottie's example and become a valuable member of the teaching team.

Although a larger youth division needs more leaders than a smaller one, the exact number and levels of leaders you have in your youth division will depend on the way you have chosen to organize it. The most familiar leaders include the teacher, the department leader, the secretary, the division coordinator and the general superintendent. Let us look at the characteristics and responsibilities of each of these leaders.

THE TEACHER

You can have the finest facilities, the newest equipment, and the best curriculum, but the single most important factor in any classroom is the teacher. Good teaching is a result of good teachers. What makes a good teacher? There are three characteristics or qualities that are basic when looking for a spiritual leader or teacher of youth.

1. *A good teacher loves God.* "How can you lead me, except you go before me?"—Anon. If a teacher is to lead others toward God, he must develop a relationship with God that would allow him to say with Paul, "Follow me even as I follow Jesus."

Think for a moment how reassuring it would be for a young person to be watching someone who models what he teaches. How comforting it is to share problems with someone who is still growing in grace. How thrilling it is to follow someone who is excited about his relationship with God.

2. *A good teacher loves young people.* Young people need to be involved with adults who are genuinely concerned about them and interested in them as individuals. And youth seem to have an uncanny ability to "spot a phony a mile away!" A teacher who loves young people will enjoy being with them and the more time he spends with them, the more learners will see and respond to his love. A teacher who only invests one hour a week soon communicates that the commitment is to the task and not to the learners themselves.

3. *A good teacher is teachable.* A good teacher is a growing

teacher. He is not satisfied with the "status quo" in his own life. He is growing in his knowledge of the Word. He is growing in his ability to live the Christian life. He is working to improve his skills as a teacher. Growth keeps him fresh, vibrant and effective as he leads his learners.

Some people are natural athletes while others have to work harder at developing their athletic skills. Some people possess a natural instinct for a good teaching style, while for others becoming a good teacher requires a lot of work. What is important is to be aware that good teaching skills can be learned, and that a good teacher can always become a better teacher.

So, how do you become a better teacher? There are four things that you can do to improve your teaching skills.

1. Read. There are many good books that can help you as a teacher. You will find a recommended list at the end of this book. As Christians we look to Jesus, the Master Teacher, for a model. He created us (and that includes the way we learn) and who should know better how to teach us? Therefore Teaching Techniques of Jesus by Herman H. Horne, is especially beneficial reading.

2. Observe. Observing a good teacher in action can help improve your own teaching skills. Seeing practical examples of principles and instructions you read about can add new insights and dimensions to your understandings. Discussing teaching techniques over coffee with a good teacher is time well invested for you and often an exciting chance for them to share.

3. Attend seminars. In-service training made available through seminars, clinics and workshops provides invaluable assistance to teachers who want to improve their skills.

4. Practice. All of the insights gained and knowledge accumulated will not automatically make a person a good teacher. You have heard the old saying "practice makes perfect." Well, it may not make "perfect," but it certainly helps. Begin by concentrating on improving only one or two teaching skills at a time. Then add other skills one at a time.

What Does a Good Teacher Do?

The responsibilities of a good teacher include, but are not limited to, the following:

1. Guides learners to spiritual growth by
   - asking the Holy Spirit for guidance
   - researching biblical truths before the session
   - determining learners' individual needs for growth
   - setting learning objectives
   - planning sessions for maximum learning
   - creating effective classroom environment for the sessions
   - keeping learners on track through instructions and questions
   - sharing the learners' excitement of discovery
   - evaluating learners' progress
   - modeling the Christian walk in his own life
2. Motivates learners to learn by
   - selecting challenging Bible learning methods
   - giving learners freedom to explore and discover God's truths
   - encouraging learners to be honest in expressing their ideas and feelings
   - assisting learners to make plans for assuming responsibility for making life changes
   - following up on learners' plans
3. One who models
   - Christ's love through his own love for students
   - how to live as a Christian through how he acts in and out of the classroom
   - the power of God's Word for daily living as he shares with students his own adventures in following Christ
   - concern for others
4. Cares for learners by
   - getting to know each learner
   - accepting learners where they are
   - listening to learners

- affirming the personal worth of each learner
- praying for each learner individually
- giving time outside of class to learners as needed
- being a real person and a real friend
- maintaining discipline in the small group
- making notes and following through to deal with questions not answered in class
- following up on absentees
- evaluating teaching effectiveness
- improving teaching skills

THE DEPARTMENT LEADER

The department leader, like a teacher, must be one who loves God, enjoys being with and investing in young people, and is open to personal growth. The department leader must also be able to work with and motivate other adults. He is responsible for directing the department teaching team.

A good department leader will want to improve both personal teaching skills and his ability to lead other adults. He will read current literature in these fields, observe successful department leaders in action when possible, attend appropriate seminars, and practice and evaluate his skills as he develops them.

One of the major responsibilities of the department leader is to guide the teachers of the department in planning the sessions they will teach together. A well-prepared department leader will have a teaching plan already outlined before the planning meeting. However, he should encourage the teachers to share their own ideas for the session plan first. He then would be wise to "offer" ideas, as suggestions, only in the areas where part of the session plan is incomplete. A department leader should encourage the teaching plan already outlined before the planning meeting. However, he should encourage the teachers to share their own ideas for the session plan first. He then would be wise to "offer" ideas, as suggestions, only in the areas where part of the session plan is incomplete. A department leader should encourage the teaching team to be creative in much the same way a teacher helps learners to be creative. If he does the work for them, creativity will be stifled.

The department leader also coordinates the sharing of the groups during the sessions. As each group shares, the department leader should affirm the learning which has occurred by praising "the ideas and not the art work." He should also show how all of the different aspects of the session topic fit together and build upon each other.

In summary, responsibilities of the department leader include, but are not limited to, the following:

1. Guides teachers as they guide learners by
   - asking for the Holy Spirit's guidance
   - researching with teachers the Bible truths before each session
   - assisting teachers in determining individual learner needs for growth
   - assisting teachers in setting learning objectives
   - coordinating the planning of the session for maximum learning
   - coordinating setting up the room arrangements and supplies
   - keeping the sessions on the time schedule planned
   - sharing with learners in their excitement of discovery
   - sharing with teachers in their excitement over learner growth
   - evaluating the learning which occurs
2. Motivates teachers to teach effectively by
   - assisting them to motivate learners in small groups
   - encouraging freedom to use new Bible learning methods and to practice new teaching skills
   - encouraging teachers to express honestly with him their criticism, suggestions, ideas and feelings
   - encouraging teachers in their own spiritual growth

3. Cares for teachers by
   - getting to know each teacher
   - accepting the teachers where they are
   - affirming the personal worth of each teacher
   - praying for each teacher individually
   - giving time outside of class to teachers as needed
   - being a real person and a real friend
   - evaluating his own effectiveness as a department leader
   - improving his own leadership skills
   - making notes of things to do and following through as needed
   - listening to teachers
   - assisting teachers with discipline when appropriate

THE SECRETARY

The secretary should be someone who is able to get along well with adults and young people. A department with loving teachers, a loving department leader, and an unpleasant secretary can have some real problems. On the other hand, a secretary who smiles and exudes warmth and love for the learners as she works and participates, provides another beautiful adult model for the young people to observe and follow.

Most youth divisions keep some type of records of such things as membership, visitors, prospects, birthdays, attendance and offerings. The record system may be as simple as checking attendance in a roll book and counting the offering, or it may be as complex as completing data processing forms. Whatever system is used, one person in each department should be given the responsibility of keeping these records. This person serves as department secretary.

Responsibilities of a secretary include, but are not limited to, the following:

1. Works with the department leader to maintain the records system

2. Warmly greets and welcomes learners
3. Registers new learners
4. Maintains accurate records
5. Receives, records, reports and submits offerings to the appropriate person
6. Studies and analyzes the records, and then reports information which may be of importance to the department leader
7. Assists in preparing absentee follow-up information
8. Assists teachers with personal follow-up and visiting from learner absentee or prospect lists.

While the secretary seldom (if ever) teaches a small group, his function is vital to the growth and success of your youth program. Therefore choose a secretary with the same prayerful care as you do any of the other members of your teaching team.

THE DIVISION COORDINATOR

Even if you have no more than two departments in the youth division, the position of division coordinator can be helpful. But, when more than three departments exist in the youth division, it is definitely advisable to have a division coordinator. A division coordinator guides and coordinates the department leaders in their work. He needs to keep the leaders of the department informed about what is going on in the total division, such as trends concerning the age group, seminars and other teacher training programs. He needs to lead in keeping the division abreast of all the newer techniques of teaching.

The division coordinator cooperates with the general superintendent in seeking out, enlisting and training department leaders, and in evaluating and coordinating the work of the departments over which he is responsible. Just as the superintendent is team leader of the teaching unit of the Sunday School, so the division coordinator is leader of a team of department leaders.

The responsibilities of a division coordinator include, but are not limited to, the following:

1. Guides department leaders by
   - asking for the Holy Spirit's guidance
   - coordinating the direction of the division and the individual departments
   - helping to set reachable departmental goals
   - responding to requests for assistance
   - assisting with evaluating the effectiveness of the departments
   - assisting to assess the needs within the departments
   - being supportive of the department leaders as they do their job
   - modeling good leadership skills as he works with the department leaders
2. Motivates department leaders by
   - assisting them to motivate teachers
   - encouraging department leaders to share their suggestions, ideas and feelings honestly with him
   - affirming department leaders as they share their own growth
3. Cares for department leaders by
   - getting to know each department leader personally
   - affirming the personal worth of each department leader
   - listening to department leaders
   - praying for each department leader individually
   - giving time to leaders as needed
   - being a real person and a real friend
   - helping maintain discipline in the division

THE GENERAL SUPERINTENDENT

All workers should be aware of the responsibilities of the general superintendent so that they can help him succeed in his task. This officer is responsible for planning, conducting and evaluating the ministry of the overall program for all age levels. He should be the one who recommends and assists in enlisting personnel when needed. He leads in setting goals for achievement. He also leads in determining training needs and in planning and directing training activities. He administers requests for and uses of financial and physical resources. He cooperates with leaders from other church organizations to coordinate a well-balanced program of Christian education.

FIGURE 1 ■ **YOUR PLACE ON THE TEAM**

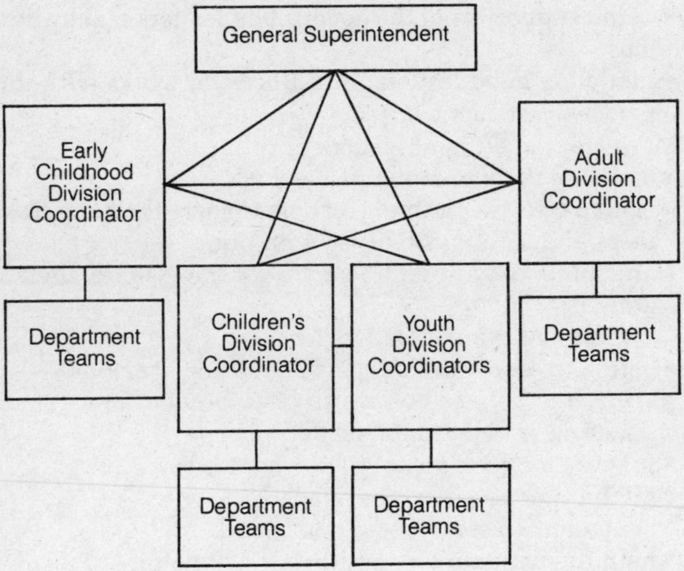

NOTE SPACE

Finding and Training Leaders

Do you read the previous chapters and sigh inside because you do not have enough leaders and do not think you ever could? Do you find yourself wondering...

HOW DO YOU FIND LEADERS?

Believe it or not, recruitment can be easy! Remember that God has gifted various members of Christ's Body for leadership. Your youth department has specific leadership needs, and God has placed in your church believers whom He has gifted for leadership. As those people are located and trained, they are enabled to exercise their gifts and minister effectively. With this in mind, build a recruitment plan using the following steps:

1. Make recruitment everyone's responsibility. Every leader in your department should be on the lookout for potential new leaders and refer names of those people to the department leader, division coordinator or general superintendent. This should provide a continual prospect list.

2. Consistently promote the teaching ministries to the congregation. Build a spirit of enthusiasm and positive image for your youth ministry by periodically sharing what is happening. Let people know God is at work. Remember, enthusiasm is catching.

Describe your leadership opportunities to your church congregation and invite interested people to talk to current leaders. If you do this consistently, instead of just when vacancies arise, the prospects can be trained in advance. This way you are prepared for unexpected vacancies and you also have more time to be sure that you fill each vacancy with just the right person.

3. Write well-defined job descriptions. A carefully designed job description needs to be developed for each position in your program. People work best when they know what is expected of them. And, people will be in a better position to know if they are interested in a job if they know what the job entails.

You may use the responsibilities outlined earlier in this chapter as a basis for writing job descriptions. However, a job description needs to be adapted for your specific needs to be most effective. If monthly reports are required, when are they due? If forms are provided for ordering supplies, reserving equipment, or keeping learner records, which forms are they and where do leaders get them?

4. Search for people with necessary qualifications. One source of people are the referrals from other leaders. Another will be the interested prospects who respond to announcements made to the congregation. (Remember that public pleas sometimes attract unqualified people. Be prepared to handle this.) Ask God to get you in touch with the leaders He has for your youth. Then get to know the adults in your church, keeping in mind that you are looking for qualified leaders. Be sensitive to clues people may give you. Be aware that some people are frightened or shy about trying something new and will need the assurance that they will be trained and given as much support as they need to develop their teaching skills. Be aware that some people may have "taught" for years in other churches and may consider themselves quite qualified but may not really understand the learning process. These people may be very motivated and with further training can be excellent teachers.

5. Secure approval of prospects through channels. Your

church probably has policies and procedures for selection and appointment of leaders. Be familiar with these and when you have discovered several prospects who indicate interest in being a leader in the youth division, be sure to secure approval of the prospects through those channels.

6. Clearly present the challenge of the job to the prospects. As you present the specific challenges of working with young people to the prospects, review the expectations of the position and answer any questions as honestly as you can.

Approach people with a positive attitude. Recruiting leaders can be exciting. Do not bog people to take on jobs because you need to fill empty spaces or because it is their duty. Do not club them with a sense of responsibility. Instead, motivate them to get excited about being part of such a miraculous ministry. Inspire them by sharing how spiritual gifts work and how God is working in the lives of young people within the department.

7. Arrange for the prospects to observe the job in action. The best way to help prospects see what their new job would be like is to arrange for them to observe (and maybe assist) for a couple of weeks in the department they might be working in. Choose the most capable teachers or department leaders to assist you in this phase of recruiting.

8. Give a prospect time for prayer and thought. Once a prospect understands the job and has observed a class in action, he should be given time for prayer and thought. Becoming a youth leader is a serious decision which should not be taken lightly. A person needs to "count the cost" of his commitment.

9. Set a deadline for an answer. Encourage a prospect to make a decision one way or another by giving them a deadline for the answer. Two weeks is usually sufficient.

10. Provide both pre-service and in-service training. Every new leader needs some orientation to your teaching ministry before taking on the responsibility for a small group, department or division. Many new leaders will also require more extensive training so they will fully understand the learning process and the effective use of Bible learning methods. In fact, most leaders need some type of training from time to time. Therefore, training is an important ingredient in your youth teaching ministry.

HOW ARE LEADERS TRAINED?

Training is never a one-time effort, or even a yearly effort. Just as you must be continually recruiting leaders even before the need arises, you must provide continual training for all your leaders. Everything changes constantly—teaching staff, learners, culture, society, methods, organization and needs. In order for your staff to meet all these changes, training must be a continuing program.

Your workers need several different kinds of training. New teachers and leaders need orientation to your organization, educational philosophy and teaching methods. Your current staff members need to upgrade their teaching skills and knowledge constantly. Some leaders will need more training than others.

1. Determine Who Needs What Training

Before you can plan training for a leader, the training need must be identified. The training needs will determine the objectives you set and the type of training you plan.

One way to determine training needs is to use a simple inventory chart for each position. Across the top list each skill required. Down the left side write the names of everyone who holds that leadership position. Each block on the matrix can then be coded to indicate the level of competence.

The chart shown is for the position of teacher and could have been completed in several ways: 1) each individual teacher may have done a self-assessment; 2) the department leader may have completed the chart for the entire department by observing and evaluating each teacher's performance; or 3) each teacher and the department leader may have completed the chart as a joint project.

FIGURE 1 ■ **TRAINING NEEDS INVENTORY**

TEACHERS \ SKILLS	Set learner objectives	Plan effective sessions	Conduct small groups	Use lecture methods	Use written methods	Use discussion methods	Use drama methods	Use art methods
Shelly								
Ted								
Sandra								
Cliff								

Full competence—no training needed
Some competence—some training needed
Little competence—immediate training needed

Once the chart is completed, each teacher knows what his own training needs are just by reading across the row with his name on it. The department leader knows the training needs of his department by reading each task column and seeing how many teachers need further training in each task area. The goal, of course, is to have all of the squares shaded in.

A word of caution is needed here. Do not automatically assume that because a leader is not doing his job right he must need training. Some people know how to do a job, but are not doing it. They need motivation, not training.

When you have identified training needs, then you are ready to set objectives.

2. Set Learning Objectives

Learning objectives for teachers are like learning objectives for learners. They state what will be learned, when it will be reached, and how it will be evaluated. Remember that objectives must be ownable, reachable and measurable.

3. Plan and Conduct the Training

Training leaders can be as simple as providing opportunities to observe and practice new skills, or can be as complex as conducting a series of formal teacher training classes. Some of the training options available include the following:

Observing and Assisting ■ The best way to orient a new teacher or leader to your teaching program is to let him observe and assist for several weeks in the department he will be working in. He can simply observe or he can help with secretarial duties. He should be included in all planning meetings for that department. After observing for a few weeks, he should join with the learners as a participant in the Bible learning methods. When he is comfortable with the procedures, he will be ready for the responsibility of a class or department. In this way you are using your experienced teachers and leaders as your trainers.

Choose the most capable teacher or department in each division for this training activity. Ask the teacher or department leader to assist you in the training ministry by accepting new teachers for observation and assisting assignments.

Departmental Planning Meetings ■ The key purpose every departmental planning meeting is to prepare for the upcoming unit of study. As teachers systematically plan each unit and each session, they learn to work together as a team. They also learn to plan good sessions effectively, to share responsibility and to personalize the lesson to meet the needs of the learners.

The departmental planning meetings are probably the best continuing training opportunity available to you. Since your leaders are already assembled on a regular basis, plan for training at every meeting!

At this time you can help staff cope with changes which affect the entire department. During these planning meetings you can change attitudes and continually upgrade the skills of your leaders. You may also clarify organizational principles and educational philosophy, and help teachers understand grouping, time procedures, session planning, adapting curriculum and the learning process.

An easy and excellent way to provide this type of training is to present a summary of the information from one chapter of a selected resource book at each planning meeting. Afterwards, you could lead a discussion on the ideas presented.

Introduce, demonstrate and practice new Bible learning methods so teachers develop new skills. Discuss and evaluate previously used methods. Discuss age-group characteristics so teachers can better understand and reach their learners.

Departmental meetings are a good place to initiate such ideas because each of the leaders has an opportunity to express ideas and opinions. They can discuss problems freely because all of them are working with the same type of learners. They can also be specific in how to deal with the problems and challenges.

If department leaders have been properly trained, they will conduct the meeting so that each teacher learns the principles and skills which go into the making of an effective teacher. As teachers practice in these meetings, they will discover and become comfortable with new teaching and planning techniques.

Divisional Level Leadership Classes ■ You can help train teachers and leaders by providing divisional level classes. You may schedule these for several consecutive nights, for several consecutive Sunday evenings or for a weekend retreat or conference. Choose the plan which best meets the needs of your leaders. Your local church supplier has resources which will be helpful in planning the training sessions.

Individualized Instruction ■ In addition to observing and assisting and attending training times, new leaders need individualized instruction. You or another trained teacher may help them with special needs or implement a special training plan you have developed. For example, you could give a new teacher an especially helpful book of your own choosing, and assign him one or two articles or chapters to read. Then meet with him to review his reading and homework he may have done. Discuss with him the concepts he has studied and how they apply to your Bible study session.

One new teacher was having problems maintaining control in the small group. So he read an article on discipline, talked over the ideas with his department leader and tried some! They worked! He could really notice a difference!

Seminars and Clinics ■ Another resource for training both new and seasoned teachers is any training conference conducted for the benefit of several churches in an area. Some cities hold yearly conferences of this type under the auspices of a local Sunday School Association.

The International Center for Learning also sponsors regional seminars and clinics to help churches train educational leadership. Founded in 1970, the International Center for Learning is dedicated to helping teachers learn to make Bible study at all ages an exciting, enjoyable, life-changing experience. These training sessions have much to offer both the new teacher and the veteran, and are designed to help both the large, well-equipped city church and the small, one-room rural mission church with limited facilities.

The cost of seminars may be paid by the individual leaders, by the church where possible, or shared by the two. The benefit teachers gain in skills acquired and revived enthusiasm is well worth the cost.

Additional Training Resources ■ You can also supplement the above training methods with these general aids:
1. Outside reading in selected Christian education books

2. Subscriptions to Christian education publications
3. Correspondence courses on teaching or other Christian education subjects
4. Christian education evening courses from a local Bible college or seminary
5. Attendance at local or regional Sunday School conventions.

4. Determine If the Training Need Was Met

After the training, be sure to evaluate what learning occurred. Was the objective met? Has the leader acquired the needed skill? If the answer is yes, he can now concentrate on his next objective. If the answer is no, further training may be needed. Keep at it until each leader has mastered the skills he requires.

Working Together

The writer of Ecclesiastes makes a profound observation when he writes, "Two are better than one because they have a good return for their labor. For if either of them falls, the one will lift up his companion. But woe to the one who falls when there is not another to lift him up" (Eccles. 4:9,10).

Whether you handle a youth Bible class all by yourself or whether you are part of a departmental team, it is important not to walk alone. Enthusiasm and motivation will build as you share the joy and challenge of teaching with a close friend. Talking over teaching ideas with a friend can provide helpful feedback and new ideas. And when you are having those moments of discouragement and frustration, that friend can encourage you to remain faithful. Finally, all teachers should have someone who is praying for their teaching ministry and their students.

WHAT IF I WORK ALONE?

Working alone in your teaching ministry does not mean you have to walk alone. Find a close friend who is willing to pray with you about your class and listen to your joys and frustrations in teaching. That special friend may be a teacher from another age level who is also "working alone." Or you might meet someone from your area at a seminar who teaches the same age students but at a different church.

Meet regularly with this special friend. Pray for each other's spiritual growth. Share your ministries. Encourage each other to attend training sessions, read books which will help you teach better, and try new things in your classes.

If you have more than five students in your class, begin looking for someone else to teach with you. When Barnabas was sent to Antioch alone to help the new Christians grow, he went and got Paul to come help him (see Acts 11:20-26). Expect your class to grow and begin now to pray for someone to share your ministry and become a real teammate.

WHAT IF I AM PART OF A TEACHING TEAM?

Many people work together in the same department, but never feel they are really a "team." How do you become a working team? Let us begin by looking at the characteristics of a good team. A team has been described as an interdependent group of people working closely together toward a common goal, agreeing upon assigned member responsibilities and standards.

Check yourself. Are your teachers and department leader really a teaching team? Or, are they just a group of people teaching in the same room?

1. *Interdependent:* Do the teachers and the department leader feel that they are dependent upon each other to effect real learning? Are there leaders who feel that they can do it alone, or do not care what the others are doing? Is criticism given each other in place of suggestions?

2. *Working closely together*: Do your teachers and department leader meet regularly to share, learn, plan and evaluate together? Are there some who do not attend the planning meetings? Team members always work closely together.

3. *Toward a common goal*: Do your teachers and the department leader agree on the overall objective of the Bible study session as being to assist learners in their spiritual growth? Do they all work together in setting session goals which are appropriate for the learners?

4. *Agreeing on responsibilities*: Do your teachers and the department leader completely understand and fulfill their individual responsibilities for each session? Nothing destroys team spirit more than having members who do not "pull their own weight" and who are not there when you need them. Do you have leaders who forget to bring the projector, who are consistently late, or who frequently do not follow up on learner plans?

5. *And standards*: Each team has standards for its members. These are the policies, procedures and rules which its members are required to follow. All team members know that these norms are set up to help the team reach its objective, and good team members follow the rules. Do you have leaders who do what they are supposed to do, but always seem to complain about the paperwork, deadlines or losing sleep to attend meetings?

Are your leaders a *teaching team*?

PLAN TOGETHER

One way to build and maintain a team spirit in your leaders is through the planning meetings (the most important being the departmental planning meeting). Planning meetings provide the opportunity for leaders to work closely together, to begin to depend on one another, and to agree upon goals, roles and standards.

You will want to be sure that the time in planning meetings is used wisely. In traditional planning meetings most of the time is given to business or inspiration. These meetings should be a time of in-depth fellowship and communication among your staff members. But to be most effective, the staff should go beyond problems, fellowship and announcements and actually work together in preparing their sessions.

Even if teachers do not work together in the same classroom, their planning can be more exciting as they share needs and problems and pray for each other. Furthermore, teachers and leaders will plan more effectively if they plan together. When they plan sessions as a team, they will stimulate each other's thinking and encourage creativity in teaching. Newer teachers can benefit from the knowledge and ability of more experienced leaders.

In these planning meetings your teachers' spiritual gifts will complement each other. Most teachers have other spiritual gifts in addition to teaching. As they plan their Bible sessions together, one teacher with the gift of exhortation may encourage a disheartened teacher who is having problems with his class. Another teacher may minister through the gift of wisdom, another knowledge, another discernment, another faith, and so on. In this way the Holy Spirit is ministering to all your leaders and teachers as they exercise their gifts with each other. That is how Christ wants His Body to function.

PLANNING FOR TEAM TEACHING

The department which teaches together must plan together. When planning together, the departmental teaching team meets about two weeks before the start of a new unit of study. The planning meeting is simplified if each teacher has already reviewed the unit and made some planning notes. These notes form a basis for discussion. Some ideas will be modified during the discussion, some discarded, and some new ideas will be thought of by working together. The team can then choose from all of the ideas when deciding the final session plans.

Assembling the needed resources, setting up the room displays, and checking the room arrangement are responsibilities which can be assigned at the department planning meeting. Sessions and methods are also discussed as a team and evaluated. Different learner responses to the same Bible learning method can be compared. Again, the pooling of ideas is a valuable help for future teaching success. Each session presents a challenge to the teacher. No two sessions need ever be alike!

SOME OPTIONS

Planning meetings are needed whether or not your youth team is organized into departments. You are not an island. You are a part of the larger teaching team for your church, part of the youth team, and part of your own department or class team. Information needs to be coordinated and disseminated on all these levels. How do you organize for that?

First, decide which of the following organizational plans most closely describes your teaching team:

Class Level: There are no departments. Each class is led by a teacher who reports directly to the general superintendent.

FIGURE 1

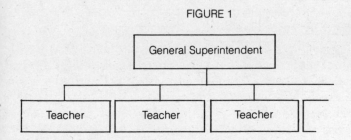

Department Level: Classes are grouped into departments. Teachers report to their department leaders, and the leaders in turn report to the general superintendent.

FIGURE 2

Division Level: The division coordinators supervise the department leaders and report to the general superintendent.

FIGURE 3

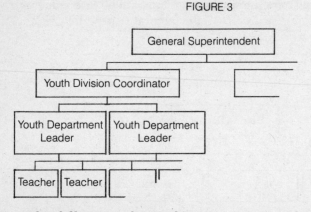

The following charts show some types of team meetings which may be helpful for your team, depending on how your teaching team is organized.

PLANNING MEETINGS FOR THE **CLASS LEVEL** YOUTH DIVISION

MEETING OF	FREQUENCY	WHO ATTENDS	AGENDA ITEMS
Sunday School Council	Quarterly (or monthly)	Conducted by the general superintendent. General superintendent and 3-5 teachers selected to represent the entire teaching staff. (Selection may be by appointment or election. Term may be from 6 months to 2 years.)	Discussion of overall calendar. Discussion of special problem areas such as personnel shortages, facility changes, record keeping. Policy setting for the Sunday School.
General Staff	Monthly immediately following the Sunday School Council meeting	Conducted by the general superintendent. General superintendent and all leaders and workers.	General announcements regarding the Sunday School calendar. Promotion of special events: e.g., graduation dates, promotion day, curriculum ordering and receiving dates, special thrusts, missionary availabilities, appreciation banquets, all-church picnics, training seminars. Report of the Sunday School Council meeting by the general superintendent.
Divisional	Monthly immediately following the general staff meeting	Conducted by a designated person at each age level. All Sunday School staff working within each age level division meet together: e.g., there will be 4 separate meetings occurring simultaneously.	Brief inspirational talk. General motivation for more effective teaching, visitation. Specific application and interpretation of information for each age level. Discussion of the details of the teaching ministry for the specific age level. Teaching improvement, ways to plan a lesson or unit. Training and practice in the use of learning activities appropriate to the specific age level. Discussion of the overall education philosophy and policies adopted by the Sunday School Council. Discussion of specific planning and teaching problems

PLANNING MEETINGS FOR THE **DEPARTMENT LEVEL** YOUTH DIVISION

MEETING OF	FREQUENCY	WHO ATTENDS	AGENDA ITEMS
Sunday School Council	Quarterly (or monthly)	Conducted by the general superintendent. General superintendent and all department leaders.	Discussion of overall calendar. Discussion of special problem areas such as personnel shortages, facility changes, record keeping. Policy setting for the Sunday School.
General Staff*	Monthly immediately following the Sunday School Council meeting.	Conducted by the general superintendent. General superintendent and all Sunday School leaders and workers.	General announcements regarding the Sunday School calendar. Promotion of special events: e.g., graduation dates, promotion day, curriculum ordering and receiving dates, special thrusts, missionary availabilities, appreciation banquets, all-church picnics and training seminars. Report of the Sunday School Council meeting by the general superintendent.
Departmental**	Monthly (weekly for best results). If monthly, immediately following the general staff meeting.	Conducted by department leaders. Each department leader meets with the secretary and teachers within his department.	Planning the unit. Planning the sessions: choosing learning methods to use, assigning specific responsibilities for the session. Discussion of and prayer about problems specific to the department. Practice with new learning activities. Training in educational philosophy specific to the age level.

*You may substitute a divisional meeting for the general staff meeting if desired. (See chart #1.)
**A department is defined as two or more classes studying the same lesson, grouped together into a department under a department leader.

PLANNING MEETINGS FOR THE **DIVISION LEVEL** SUNDAY SCHOOL

MEETING OF	FREQUENCY	WHO ATTENDS	AGENDA ITEMS
Sunday School Council	Quarterly (or monthly)	Conducted by the general superintendent. General superintendent and division coordinators.	Discussion of overall calendar. Discussion of special problem areas, such as personnel shortages, facility changes, record keeping. Policy setting for the Sunday School.
Divisional	Monthly immediately following the Sunday School Council meeting.	Conducted by division coordinators. All staff working within each age level division meet together: e.g., there will be four separate meetings occurring simultaneously. Or, division coordinators meet with their department leaders, who then relay the information to teachers during the department meeting.	Brief inspirational talk. General motivation for more effective teaching, visitation. Specific application and interpretation of information for each age level. Discussion of the details of the teaching ministry for the specific age level. Teaching improvement, ways to plan a lesson or unit. Training and practice in the use of learning activities appropriate to the specific age level. Discussion of the overall education philosophy and policies adopted by the Sunday School Council. General announcements and promotions.
Departmental*	Monthly (weekly for best results). If monthly, immediately following the divisional meeting.	Conducted by department teachers. Each department leader meets with the secretary and teachers within his department.	Planning the unit. Planning the sessions: choosing learning methods to use, assigning specific responsibilities for the session. Discussion of and prayer about problems specific to the department. Practice with new learning activities. Training in educational philosophy specific to the age level.

*A department is defined as two or more classes all studying the same lesson, grouped together into a department under a department leader.

OK. Now you know who are the leaders in the youth division, and what each leader should be doing. You have some ideas for recruiting and training leaders. And, you are using the planning meetings to build a teaching team effectively. Now what?

EVALUATE FOR EFFECTIVENESS

Most of us agree that good planning is important. "Set objectives," we say. "If you don't know where you are going, how will you know when you have arrived?" So we set objectives and make our plans. We also agree that implementing our plans is important; "The best plan is no good if you don't use it." So we get to work. And we usually see progress.

Some of us stop there! And some of us subsequently fail because we forgot to check our progress, to evaluate for needed improvements, and to anticipate so we can handle unexpected problems which arise. Taking time to evaluate progress can be the key to success. Furthermore, evaluating helps us grow and improve—and growing together helps us grow in team spirit. But who evaluates what?

The Teacher Evaluates...

The teacher (or small group leader) evaluates his teaching effectiveness by checking some observable outcomes:

■ Are learners finishing their assignments too quickly, or not at all? Why? Why not?
■ Are learners paying attention during the small group time? Why? Why not?
■ Are learners setting good goals for implementing in their lives during the week what they study?
■ Is there problem behavior within the small group? If so, what are the causes? What changes are needed?
■ Do I have a good relationship with the young people within the group? How could I improve?
■ Am I following up on learner plans during the week?

The Department Leader Evaluates...

The department leader (or lead teacher) evaluates his department effectiveness by checking some observable outcomes:

- Is the noise level within the department high enough but not too high, during the small group times?
- Are learners involved with what is happening in their small groups?
- Are learners in some groups looking around the room instead of paying attention to their teacher?
- Is there a learner making a disturbance in any of the small groups?
- Are any of the teachers signaling for assistance?
- Are some of the teachers seemingly doing all of the talking within the small groups?
- Do all of the teachers have good relationships with their teens?
- Can all of the teachers ask for assistance when they need it?
- Can all of the teachers accept suggestions?
- Do all of the teachers attend and participate in the planning meetings?

The Division Coordinator Evaluates...

The division coordinator evaluates the effectiveness of each of his departments, using the same criteria that the department leader uses to evaluate his staff.

Everyone Evaluates Together...

Evaluation should be extended to every part of the program. Therefore all of the youth division staff together evaluate the following kinds of details:

1. *The facilities:* equipment, room design, which classes are assigned to which classrooms, lighting, temperature, need for painting or repairs.

2. *The communications:* laterally—between the various staff members; upwards—from learners to teachers, teachers to department leader and others; and downwards—from the general

superintendent to the department leaders and on down to the teachers and others.

3. *The staffing ratios:* Are the classes the best size? Are the department leaders supervising from one to five teachers? Are the divisional coordinators over one to five department leaders?

4. *The leaders:* Are the leaders satisfied with their "assignments"? Are there problems which need to be discussed? What about the working relationships?

5. *The sessions:* Are there problems? Should the session be lengthened, the order of the blocks of time be switched, the responsibilities changed?

6. *The curriculum:* Is the current curriculum still meeting the need? Are the illustrations appropriate? Is the content at the proper level for the learners?

7. *The planning meetings:* Are they frequent enough, conducted correctly, covering the right material, a waste of time? Are enough leaders in attendance? Should the meeting date be changed?

8. *The training:* Is more needed than is being provided? Is a different type of training needed? Who should conduct the training? Which type of training seems to be the most effective?

9. *The attendance:* Which classes show a high rate of absenteeism? Why? What percent of the overall youth division enrollment is in regular attendance? How can the percentage be increased? How can the enrollment be increased?

10. *The interest:* Do the learners seem interested in the classes? Which methods do they like best? Which methods do they seem to learn the most from? How is the interest shown?

11. *Objectives:* What things should the sessions accomplish? How? When? In what way and to what degree? Do you want to continue with the same basic objectives or do you feel you should change the emphasis of the Bible school in your own church?

These items are only suggestions. You will need to evaluate

your program to check its effectiveness, its efficiency, where the needs are and where to set new goals. You must decide what evaluative device will be most useful for you. Check the statistics, solicit feedback from the staff and the learners, set specific, measurable short-term goals, and start now!

When to Evaluate

If a problem arises, you will of course evaluate the cause and possible solutions right then. But the major items in the program also need periodic evaluation.

For example, you might evaluate the space assignments, curriculum and leaders once a year—probably a few months before promotion and the new "year" starts. For most churches, the new year starts in September, concurrent with the beginning of the secular school year. So plan the evaluation for the summer so that you allow enough time to initiate changes as a result of the evaluation.

Short-term goals should be set on a quarterly basis for most projects. Therefore, you should evaluate them every quarter and set new goals or extend the time on the current ones.

Evaluating is like mowing the lawn. If you keep it up, it is not too much of a problem, but if you let it go, the task becomes monumental!

SUCCESS

The success of a youth Sunday School is no accident! Success is only possible if the leaders join together with each other and the Holy Spirit to form a real *teaching team*.

PART 4 BIBLE LEARNING METHODS

USING BIBLE LEARNING METHODS EFFECTIVELY

SOME METHODS YOU CAN USE

Using Bible Learning Methods Effectively

"What is a Bible learning method? Is it a poem, a poster, a skit? Is it used to fill up the time?"

These are valid questions asked by many teachers who are not sure what relationship the use of different Bible learning methods has to the "teaching of the lesson."

A Bible learning method can be described as any assignment which prepares the learner or leads the learner to examine God's Word and better understand His point of view or how He would have His people live. Bible learning methods can be extremely effective teaching tools, and they need to be chosen with as much care and thoughtfulness as when choosing a tool in building a fine piece of furniture or repairing an automobile.

The careful choice and use of Bible learning methods will help you create greater learner interest and motivation. The right methods will get your learners involved in the learning process and take them from the role of passively listening to one of actively digging into the Scriptures. The proper methods help create the desire to explore and study intensely in order to examine and evaluate information, synthesize ideas and draw conclusions, all based on God's Word. Bible learning methods can also be used to motivate the learner to make practical applications of the truths being studied as he wrestles with their relevancy for day-to-day living.

EXAMPLES OF BIBLE LEARNING METHODS

Listed below are several examples that demonstrate ways in which Bible learning methods can be used in each part of the Bible session.

Approach

Three examples of ways to use Bible learning methods during the Approach part of the session are:

1. Turn to a person sitting next to you and share with him the last time someone went out of his way to do something kind for you. (Neighbor-nudge)

2. Help me list on the chalkboard as many manifestations of the occult as you are aware of. (Brainstorm)

3. "The actions of any one Christian do not seriously affect other Christians" (written on a chalkboard or poster). Those of you who agree with the statement, stand on this side of the room and those who disagree stand on the other side of the room. We will take five minutes to exchange ideas and try to persuade the other side to change their position. (Agree-Disagree)

Note: Notice that while reading your Bible is not necessary to complete these instructions, they do prepare the learner to consider the good Samaritan in number 1, Simon the Sorcerer, in number 2 and 1 Corinthians 10 in number 3.

Bible Exploration

These are three examples of ways to use Bible learning methods during the Bible Exploration part of the session:

1. Based on Luke 10:30-37, use your imagination to write a letter from the victim to his cousin sharing what happened and also his feelings. (Letter Writing)

2. Based on 1 Thessalonians chapter 2, list desirable characteristics for Christians who minister to others. Make a second list of undesirable characteristics. (List)

3. To help you explain the significance of John 3:14,15 prepare a poster illustrating the two events to which Jesus is referring.

See Numbers 21:5-9 and Luke 23:33,39-43 for additional insights. (Drawing)

Note: It would be difficult to complete any of these instructions without first digging into God's Word. These instruct the learner to gather information and evaluate it. After researching, the learners should be able to state and discuss what God is saying in the Scripture passages indicated.

Life Exploration

Here are three examples of directions for Bible learning methods for the Life Exploration part of the session:

1. Based on what you learned from Luke 9:23, write a modern-day story that illustrates some possible costs of following Jesus today. (Parallel Story)

2. Based on what you learned from Luke 10:25-37, prepare a skit that would illustrate opportunities teenagers have to be good Samaritans today. (Skit)

3. Based on James 3:13-18, write a song that expresses the importance of acquiring God's wisdom. (Song)

Note: These instructions will help learners think through present day applications of Scripture passages.

Conclusion-Decision

Two ways to use Bible learning methods during the Conclusion-Decision part of the session are:

1. Write a tanka poem that expresses to God your thankfulness for making His wisdom available. A tanka has five lines with 5,7,5,7,7 syllables in each line respectively. (Tanka Poem)

2. In the light of what you have learned in today's Bible study, complete one of the following sentences:

  a. This week I want to _____

  b. When I pray this week, I will ask the Lord to _____

  c. If I could share with a friend the one key thing I have learned today, it would be _____

(Sentence Completion)

ONE METHOD CAN BE USED MANY WAYS

Sometimes it is easy to associate certain methods with a particular part of the session. Just because the examples in this book use particular Bible learning methods with specific parts of the session, do not let that restrict your concept of how those methods can be used. Most Bible learning methods can be used in a variety of ways. For example, consider how "writing a prayer" could be used at each part of the session:

For the *Approach*: The leader begins by telling a story. "A Christian teenager has been ordered by his school principal to stop sharing his faith on campus. After leaving the principal's office, the student stops to pray. Write what you think you would pray in that situation. Allow time for writing, then guide the learners into the lesson.

For the *Bible Exploration*: After reading Acts 3:1-11, write a prayer the healed man might have prayed after entering the Temple.

For the *Life Exploration*: Write a prayer of thanks from a teenager who has just received Christ as Saviour.

For the *Conclusion-Decision*: Write a short prayer to God asking for specific help with a specific problem that you are willing to commit to Him this week.

WRITE CLEAR INSTRUCTIONS

Making instructions clear and to the point will make the task easier and more productive for the learners. Instructions should be step-by-step and tell the learner specifically what is required. Do not say, "Discuss the passage." Instead say, "Answer the following questions..." If you are looking for five main points, tell the learner. The more precise you are with your instructions, the more successful your activities will be. Whenever possible, instructions should also be practiced on someone else for clarity before the Bible session and put in written form.

VARIETY AND SELECTIVITY ARE KEYS

What is the best method?

1. *The method you did not use last week!* This is a big key in maintaining the interest of young people

2. *A method learners are able to do.* Do not ask poor readers to read long passages silently and answer questions. They need short passages, read out loud, and discussed. Do not ask seventh grade boys to do a lot of writing. Because of poor small muscle coordination writing is often difficult and therefore uninteresting. Make sure there is adequate time to complete tasks. (You may misjudge once in a while. But do not let it be habitual.)

3. *A method which is appropriate for the content.* The goal is Bible research and discussion of life issues. The method is only a way to make that study more interesting and involving.

MAKING IT HAPPEN

But what if learners have difficulty with the assignment? What if the group is not excited about doing that particular assignment? What if it is "over their head"?

If the difficulty seems to lie in understanding the instructions, ask someone in the group to explain them to you. In this way you will have a much clearer perception as to where the trouble lies.

If they balk at the method (chances are they will not, if you are excited about it!), ask them to try it and evaluate its worth after completion. Assure them that if they still feel the same way that you will try to avoid using it again in the future.

If they seem to have difficulty understanding the Scripture passage or properly expressing what they have discovered, the teacher's wise use of questions will be most helpful here.

ASKING THE RIGHT QUESTIONS

Fortunately the creative teacher does not have to be skilled in all the arts of group dynamics in order to use Bible learning methods successfully. But learning how to use questions as a teaching tool can be of inestimable value to a teacher, particularly questions designed to make the learners think. Well thought-out questions will help learners to identify and evaluate information, to interpret it, and to assess how that information affects their value structures and decision making.

How to Choose Your Questions

1. Questions should require the learner to think. Avoid asking questions which may be answered with only yes or no.

2. Keep the questions brief and simple, restricting each question to one main thought.

3. Distinguish between a question asking for facts and one seeking opinions.

4. Avoid asking questions which the group cannot answer.

5. The questions should be a natural part of the presentation, not something artificially tacked on at the end.

6. The tone and manner of your questions should encourage the learners to express themselves. A friendly, pleasant and sincere tone of voice will encourage confidence and understanding.

Keeping in mind these basic characteristics of questioning, let us consider three different types of questions.

Informational Questions

An informational question requires the learner to remember specific facts in order to answer the question correctly. Informational questions also enable a teacher to discern how well a learner knows the basic facts about a given situation or Bible passage.

Examples: Where did Moses live as a child? To what country did Moses flee after killing the Egyptian? How long did Moses stay in the desert?

It is almost impossible to have a meaningful discussion guided by informational questions alone. Therefore, we also need analytical questions.

Analytical Questions

Analytical questions encourage learners to attach meaning to the facts. Questions of this type are more open-ended than informational questions. By using these, the teacher helps learners share what they understand and perceive about the facts.

Examples: What are some reasons why Moses would be reluctant to return to Egypt? What do you think Moses meant when he said...?

Personal Questions

Personal questions seek out a learner's values and attitudes. Questions at this level are an effective means for engaging learners in the process of reflecting, expressing and acting on concerns that relate to them personally. The focus of these questions is to guide learners in their own decision making and value forming.

Examples: If you had been Moses, what would you have done when...? How would you decide what would be the right thing to do in this situation?

TWO LAST TIPS

Sometimes in presenting the results of study, students do not clearly convey the main points. The wise teacher will learn to discern when this has happened and in no more than one or two sentences summarize the main points for the class after sharing.

Also, transitions between each of the learning methods will help students better understand how the overall lesson fits together and will focus students' thoughts on the objectives. These transitions should be short and concise: "We have studied three ways Jesus showed love to people. Now let's look at what we can do to show love to others." This lets students know where you are going so they can work *with* you to reach your objectives.

Some Methods You Can Use

In chapter 10 we have described the function of Bible learning methods, given examples of how instructions for their use can be written for each part of the session, and how the teacher can use questions to aid the learners in their search for understanding. Now let us explore some specific methods you might use. This is not an exhaustive list, but only the beginning. The following Bible learning methods have been grouped into seven major categories: Discussion, Writing, Drama, Art, Music, Lecture and Audiovisuals.

■ DISCUSSION

There is probably no more potentially valuable method of teaching than discussion. A discussion that is carefully planned and skillfully directed can change an ordinary class session into an exciting and lively learning experience.

Sometimes a teacher will try a discussion and fail, vowing never to use that method again. Or the teacher may be fearful of the questions that might be raised and therefore never even make the effort to try. Unfortunately, the students of such teachers miss the opportunity to internalize facts, ideas, and concepts and to wrestle with their meanings.

A discussion has been defined as "a cooperative search for truth as the group seeks solutions to a problem or question." There is interaction between teacher and students and between student and student. The learning leader is there to be a resource and a guide to keep things going.

The best physical arrangement for discussion is a circle, which allows members of the group to see each other. The beginning of the discussion may sound more like a question-answer session, with the teacher addressing questions to the group, and answers given back to the teacher. But if the questions are phrased in a way that solicits opinions on the issue involved, the group will start responding to each other's statements and the discussion will start rolling. There must be a debatable issue involved. It just does not work to try and start a discussion on a point or issue where everyone is in agreement.

Even if you have an issue, sometimes youth may be in a mood that stifles good discussion, and you never get past the question-answer phase. Be patient and go on with the session as planned, and if you keep an atmosphere of openness and acceptance, your students will eventually open up. Avoid putting them down by criticizing their lack of response.

The teacher should carefully plan the discussion questions so answers will have to be more than yes or no. Have another question ready in case students do not understand the first question, be prepared to reword it, or ask a learner to rephrase your question: "What do you hear me asking?" This is not the time to lecture, so keep questions and comments short and to the issue.

Another way to stimulate discussion is to show a picture and have the young people tell a story about what is happening in the picture. Several may suggest different ideas, or they may agree on one. This can lead into discussion of feelings, situations, biblical principles or other matters.

Once the discussion begins, the teacher keeps the discussion on the track. Occasionally, you may find it necessary to ask a "happy wanderer" tactfully how his comments apply to the topic. Be careful not to appear shocked when he has an answer for you.

The teacher should be sensitive to those not participating. In striving for balanced involvement, he might seek to draw the quiet members into the discussion unless it would embarrass them.

At times, the teacher might quickly summarize the discussion to that point, or ask one of the members of the group to give a summary. At the end of the discussion, a summary should be stated, along with possible conclusions. If no agreement was reached, then a restatement of the issue and various possible conclusions might be given as a summary of the session.

The main objective of a discussion is to encourage the group members to express their opinions. These opinions are open to change as other opinions are expressed and the discussion continues. Students need the assurance that they can express what they feel without getting blasted out of their chair by the teacher. Teachers are to encourage expression as the beginning of learning, and then trust the Holy Spirit to change students when necessary.

The following are some specific discussion techniques:

Agree-Disagree

Agree-disagree statements differ from true-false in that they are usually ambiguous enough that there are no absolute answers. The method is designed to generate discussion and interest, not to settle issues.

Agree-disagree statements can be either written on a chalkboard or passed out on sheets of paper. After time has been given for learners to decide if they agree, discussion begins. One interesting way to stimulate the discussion is to ask the learners to stand on opposite sides of the room: the "agrees" on one side and the "disagrees" on the other side. (No standing in the middle!) The learners are then to try to persuade their opponents to change their views.

Example: Agree or Disagree: Jesus felt that it was bad for a man to have great wealth. After 10 minutes of animated discussion and much crossing over, one group of junior highers was actually eager to discover through the Scripture, Jesus' attitude toward money. (Approach)

Brainstorming

The leader presents a problem or a question to the group. The members of the group are to respond quickly with all answers or solutions that come to mind. It does not matter how appropriate the response may be. The object is to say what comes to mind and have someone write it down on the chalkboard, paper, newsprint or overhead projector.

No evaluation is made of any response at this time, even though some responses may seem far off base. One absurd remark might trigger an idea from someone else which may turn out to be the best response.

The teacher should set a time limit for brainstorming, such as three minutes or five minutes. When the time limit is up, or when the responses slow down, the brainstorming stops and the evaluating begins.

If you have been brainstorming a problem or doing some planning, you might begin by eliminating the least valuable answers or ideas. Then evaluate the remaining suggestions in order of importance or arrange them in categories. After they are arranged, the group might consider how to put into effect the ideas suggested or apply the solutions offered.

Example: Brainstorm for one minute problems young people face today. Then select from the list the five that are most pressing. (Approach)

Can of Worms

A Can of Worms is a can containing slips of paper with squirmy questions. No easy, pat answers for these exist. Real life dilemmas often are good sources.

An empty coffee can with several of these questions which relate to the Bible passage lends an air of expectation and excitement to the session as an individual reaches in to pull out a question.

Example: A student whom you are trying to get to go to church with you asks you to keep a secret and then tells you he stole the answers for a coming exam. What will you do? Why? (*Life Exploration*)

Circle Response

The teacher proposes a question to the members of the group. Each person is called on to give his response in turn (around the circle). No one can respond to any person's statement until his turn comes again. This can be used to have each member of the group state either his understanding of the question or his response to the question. The teacher may also call for a vote as to which side of the issue the person identifies with. The statements should not be addressed to any particular person, but might be imagined as being tossed into a "ballot box" in the center of the circle.

This is a simple method with several uses. It is especially valuable when the subject is somewhat controversial or when someone has dominated the discussion and you want to give an opportunity for others to participate. Circle response is also useful when a discussion gets rather hot and the teacher feels he is losing control.

This method is valuable in providing an opportunity for each member to participate by contributing his opinion. It also gives an opportunity for each member to consider the opinions of the others since he cannot respond until his turn comes again, or the discussion is reopened. It is a method that the teacher should have close at hand to use when needed. It can also be used to open up discussion on a question.

Film Talk-back

There is an increasing number of short discussion films available at moderate rental price (or on a free loan basis from public libraries) which would provide excellent discussion starters for youth. Many filmstrips are designed for the same purpose, or for presenting information about a particular subject. The distinctive feature of the film talk-back is that it always provides for a response on the part of the viewers.

In planning a film or filmstrip, the departmental learning leader should arrange the room so that everyone has a good view of the screen. He should also be sure the equipment is in working order. Time spent making sure that everything is prepared will pay dividends during the presentation.

Before using any film or filmstrip, preview it carefully. If more than one person will be involved in leading the discussion, have them preview the film. This will also assist you in introducing the film to the group. It is most helpful to the learners if you let them know what it is they are to look for in the film. Nothing dampens the learning experience more than for the leader to introduce the film with, "I don't know what the film is about, but we're supposed to look at it, so here goes."

When previewing the film, use the discussion guide that comes with it to help you frame some questions to pose to the group to consider while viewing the film. (If no guide is available, construct questions on your own.) Following the actual showing of the film these questions will provide the basis for discussion groups. If the meaning of the film or filmstrip is not clear to the group, you might consider showing it again. Some films or filmstrips are designed to be stopped at a certain point for discussion and then started again at that point. When this is suggested, it is a good idea to follow this format for involvement. (It is also wise for the projectionist to practice this procedure in advance.) Other films will be shown straight through but the leader should have some plan for group response.

Neighbor-nudge

The Neighbor-nudge is a short discussion technique used to get all learners involved in discussion quickly. The leader asks learners to pair off in twos to discuss a question (one without a yes or no answer). Since people merely turn to the person next to them, there is seldom the need to move chairs. Furthermore, this technique provides an opportunity for each member of the group to be faced with the issue and to respond.

The teacher does not move among the groups, but is available for clarifying the problem if necessary. Discussion is usually limited to one or two minutes for a neighbor-nudge. Longer discussions are called diad discussions. At the end of the neighbor-nudge several volunteers are usually asked to share insights and ideas.

Problem Solving

In problem solving learners work together to solve an assigned problem, usually involving relationships with God or with others. This method is often a good way to give learners an opportunity to apply scriptural truths to life situations without suffering the real consequences at stake. It gives them an opportunity to consider options and the possible results so that they will be better prepared for future conflicts. Open-ended stories, situations from newspaper accounts, and even "Dear Abby" questions are good sources for consideration.

An interesting variation might be to have two solutions written by the learners. One group might write a solution they think their friends would offer and the second group might write a solution that they think a specific Bible character (Peter, John or whoever best fits with the passage they are studying) would offer. Then both groups compare the two solutions.

Question and Answer

The teacher prepares questions for the learners to answer during the Bible study. (See chapter 10 for pointers on good questions.) Learners can work alone, in groups of two or three, or as a large group to answer the questions.

A variation might be for the learners to work in small groups preparing their own questions from the passage with which they can quiz each other or the other small groups.

■ CREATIVE WRITING

You will be amazed at what your learners can create in writing when given the right assignment. Even though they might protest that they are not writers, if given the opportunity and inspiration, they will produce some very interesting, exciting and revealing results. (Learners may write individually or in groups.)

Acrostic

An acrostic is a list of words or phrases in which the first, last or other particular letters in each line, taken in order, spell a word or phrase.

Example: Write an acrostic for HAPPY. One group wrote:

H elpful
A ble to love
P rayerful
P ositive
Y oked together with Jesus (*Approach*)

Contemporary Parallel Story

Students are asked to write a contemporary story which parallels the events of biblical narrative or which illustrates the application of certain biblical principles. This method is almost always used for Life Exploration and is designed to see how learners will apply what they learned in Bible Exploration.

Example: Write modern-day story that illustrates the principle of the Good Samaritan. (*Life Exploration*)

Crossword Puzzle

This is a creative way to have students list the main points in a passage—especially when there are two lists.

Example: Prepare a list of key words and concepts from James

3:13-18 that deal with heavenly and earthly wisdom. Use the list to construct a crossword puzzle. Place words that relate to heavenly wisdom down and words that relate to earthly wisdom across. (*Bible Exploration*)

Diary, Log, Journal

The learners read the assigned passage, then try to put themselves in the place of the suggested character. They use their imaginations to write a page that the person might have written in his diary, log or journal that day. The biblical text provides the basic information, and the learners use their own judgments to fill in details of inner thoughts, feelings, responses and conclusions. The imaginary entry need not be long, but it should lead the learners to deeper thought about the events of the passage and what their Bible character felt and experienced. There are no ready-made, right-or-wrong answers, so he must actually think and this helps him realize that Bible people were real people. Notice that girls write diaries but boys keep logs and journals.

Example: Based on Luke 10:25-37 write a page in the inn-keeper's diary (log, journal). (*Bible Exploration*)

Letter Writing

The learners read the assigned passage and then try to put themselves in the place of the suggested character. They use their imaginations to write a letter that the person might have written that day. The biblical text provides the basic information, and the learners use their own judgments to fill in details of inner thoughts, feelings, responses and conclusions.

As with the diary writing, the imaginary letter need not be long, but it should lead the learners to deeper thought. There are no ready-made, right-or-wrong answers, so they must actually think, just as with the diary assignment.

Examples: Based on Luke 10:25-37 write a letter from the victim to a cousin in Joppa relating his experiences and feelings. (*Bible Exploration*)

Or, write a letter to a teenager encouraging him to be helpful to others as an expression of Jesus' love. (*Life Exploration*)

List

Students can be asked to work alone or in groups to list almost any kind of information. Asking learners to list key facts or concepts from a Scripture passage is a very straightforward way to involve them in a Scripture search.

Examples: List all the positive traits for discipleship you can find in 1 Thessalonians 2:1-13. (*Bible Exploration*) Or, list ways Christian teens could demonstrate those traits with others today. (*Life Exploration*) Or, list three things you will do to improve family relationships this week. (*Conclusion-Decision*)

Litany

In a litany the group decides on a standard refrain. Then between each refrain said by the group, a member of class prays a one-sentence or one-thought prayer.

Example: If the learners are to write a litany of praise and thanksgiving on salvation, they might choose "Thank you for salvation, dear Lord" as the refrain. The litany might sound like this:

Individual: What great love you showed on the cross,
Group: Thank you for salvation, dear Lord.
Individual: I was such a sinner and in need of help,
Group: Thank you for salvation, dear Lord.
Etc. (*Conclusion*)

Open-ended Stories

These are situations printed on a sheet of paper with space left for the student to finish the story. The teacher presents the case with the background material and different factors involved. Then the story is given to the student. He reads the story, which just happens to break off at the crucial point. The learner's task is to finish the story, working out the situation.

When finished, the learner shares his "ending" with the class and also responds to the contributions of the other group members. The value of this experience is increased if the teacher will briefly summarize the various solutions presented and ask for some possible applications of the principles discussed. Open-ended stories are usually used in Life Exploration.

Example: When Sue came home, bringing her friend Fran along, she planned to ask her mother if she could go bicycle riding. Fran had a new 10-speed she wanted to show to Sue. Some older boys were going to meet them at the park so they could all ride around together. But Sue's mother wasn't home. She had left a note asking Sue to stay at home and start dinner. Fran urges Sue to come out and ride bikes anyway. She tells her she can probably get home in time to start supper. What will Sue do? (*Life Exploration*)

Outline

Ask your learners to make an outline for a Scripture passage. This will help them to synthesize and evaluate what they are reading.

Example: Outline Paul's sermon in Acts 17:22-31. (*Bible Exploration*)

Paraphrase

Paraphrasing a passage (stating the meaning of a passage in his own words) will emphasize the ability of the learner to interpret and express in his own words the Bible passage and helps identify concepts which are not clearly understood. Furthermore, the paraphrase becomes a very personal expression. A paraphrase assignment is usually most appropriate during the *Bible Exploration* phase of the lesson.

Example: Write the plan of salvation by paraphrasing Romans 3:23; Romans 5:8; John 1:12; John 3:16; and Romans 10:13.

One learner paraphrased these verses this way: "I have sinned and do not measure up to God's standards. But, God showed His great love for me while I was still a sinner, by sending Christ to die for me. And if I receive Him, God will give the power to become His child. All I have to do is trust God and believe in Christ. When I believe, I will live forever, because whoever calls out to God will be saved!"

Poetry

There are many forms of poetry, from lines written in metered rhyme to free flowing expressions of thoughts and feelings. Three special kinds of poetry that you may wish to consider are the psalm, haiku and tanka.

The psalm may be a series of couplets which first make a statement and then repeat the statement in slightly different words (e.g., Ps. 71:1-3), a series of thoughts which include an often repeated refrain (eg., in Ps. 136), or just a general poem expressing worship and praise to God.

The haiku is a brief Japanese verse of 17 syllables, arranged in three lines of 5, 7 and 5 syllables. *Example:* God is my refuge. He is my strength and help. I will praise His name. *(Conclusion)*

The tanka is a Japanese verse of 31 syllables arranged in five lines of 5,7,5,7 and 7 syllables. *Example:*

To follow Jesus
Among friends who reject Him
Is no simple task.
But in trusting Him comes strength
To be a strong disciple. *(Life Exploration)*

Research and Report

There are several ways to use this method. One is to give individual research assignments to be carried out between class sessions. The assignment can range from a series of interviews to a study of books and periodicals. Or an individual might be assigned to visit an institution to learn how the youth can be involved in service there.

When planning individual assignments, a problem is presented to the group. Then specific assignments are given to individual members. The time (usually the next meeting) is specified for reporting the results of the research.

Another variation involves giving assignments to small groups or teams. These are researched during the week, or possibly during the class session. The latter would require the teacher to have resource materials available in the classroom.

For example, the class might come to a passage of Scripture with several possible interpretations. The class is divided into research teams, each given several commentaries and Bible dictionaries. Each team is given an assignment which they research. After time for study, small groups are reconvened into the one larger group and reports are given by each research team. The teacher then summarizes the results of the reports.

Another variation is the book report. Related novels or biographies are assigned to different individuals, who give a report to the large group at the appropriate time in the unit study.

TV Script

Writing a TV script is similar to writing a newspaper report except students present the results in dramatic form. This often creates more interest and is remembered longer.

Example: Write a TV script of a news show based on Judges 6. (This Bible Exploration assignment can be divided among different small groups.)

    verses 1-6—Financial report
    verses 7-10—Religious news
    verses 11-24—International news
    verses 25-32—Local news
    verses 33-35—National news
    verses 36-40—Weather

Write a Newspaper Article or Story

In this method, the learner or a small group of learners write a newspaper article based on the assigned text. The article should be written as it might have appeared in a newspaper the day after the event. It might be written from an objective point of view as a straight news item, or as an editorial giving personal opinions and evaluations.

The article need not be long, but it should include as many facts—who, what, where, when, why and how—as possible. The sentences should be short and concise, the headline chosen appropriately. In some cases the biblical text will provide all the material needed to fill in details of what led up to the event or what followed. In other cases the learners will need to use their imagination to fill in details around the information given. This method helps learners to get involved in the biblical narrative and understand the people as real human beings like themselves.

Example: Based on Jesus' cleansing of the Temple (John 2:13-16), write a banner headline and the lead article for the *Jerusalem Journal*. (*Bible Exploration*)

Or, write a headline and lead article for a school newspaper about a student ordered not to share his faith at school. (*Life Exploration*)

Write a Prayer

This is similar to letter writing. Writing prayers helps students focus on the importance of discussing with God all aspects of daily living.

Example: Based on Luke 10:25-37 write a prayer the priest in the parable might pray about the man by the road when he arrives at the Temple. (*Bible Exploration*)

Or, write a prayer a tenth grader might pray who is having difficulty in living for Christ at school. (*Life Exploration*)

Telephone Number

Many students can remember telephone numbers more easily than Scripture references. Capitalize on this by having them list important references as telephone numbers.

Example: Make up a telephone number from the key Scripture references. One group wrote: "Worried about the future? Call MT 6-3133"—translation: Matthew 6:31,33. (*Bible Exploration or Life Exploration*)

■ **DRAMA**

With drama, the material comes to life for the learners. It can be either a well-planned production of a written play, or a spontaneous production created almost on the spot.

Dialogue

A dialogue is a conversation between two or more persons.

Example: Prepare a dialogue between the Levite and his wife after he arrived home on the night of Luke 10:25-37. (*Bible Exploration*)

Drama/Skit

Following the study of a story or narrative in Scripture, drama makes the account come alive. Plans are made in small groups; then the dramas are presented to the large group. You need to allow sufficient time for both the planning and the presentations if you use this method. It often helps to put a time limit on the length of the drama to be presented. If you say, "Create a two-minute skit...," students will usually create skits two to five minutes long. Be prepared for this.

Examples: One group of junior highs was studying the book of Acts. When they came to the account of Saul's conversion, they decided to review the references to Saul earlier in the study as well as in this lesson, and then to act out the events in his life leading up to his conversion and his encounter with Ananias. They chose three scenes: one when Stephen was stoned, another on the road to Damascus, and the third in the room with Ananias. After 20 minutes discussing plans in the small groups, they met together to present the scenes. (*Bible Exploration*)

Another group of junior highs, when asked to present a modern-day version of the Ananias and Sapphira event, came up with some interesting ideas. One suggested a group of fellows working to raise money to send other kids to camp. The group raised $30 and gave it to one of their members to turn in to the youth director. But he only turned in $20. What happens when the others find out? (*Life Exploration*)

Interview

Interviews are easy to do. The learners read the Bible passage assigned to them and then think of how an interviewer might approach the persons included in the incident and what questions he would ask. (Most learners have seen television interviews, so they will find this method easy to work with.) The learners then determine the answers the interviewed person might give. In some cases they will find a direct basis for both question and answer in the text. In other cases, they may have to apply their own judgment and imagination to the text to determine answers. There is no right or wrong here, so no learner needs to feel threatened about this type of work. Again, suggest a time limit for the dramatized interview they are preparing.

Example: Prepare a series of interviews for the "Man on the Street" segment of the local TV News. Find out what happened in the Temple today (read John 2:13-16) and how they feel about it. (*Bible Exploration*)

Monologue

Monologue is a speech by one person. In preparing a monologue students should consider events, thoughts, feeling, questions, responses, etc., of the person they are portraying.

Example: Ask one of your learners to assume the character of the Samaritan woman in John 4 and have the other learners help that learner prepare to tell others what her innermost thoughts were. (*Bible Exploration*)

Another group might do the same for one of the disciples and yet another group for one of the townspeople who came to meet Jesus. (*Bible Exploration*)

Puppets

Learners can use chairs, table edges or blackboards for a stage front. They should then use puppets to act out a Bible drama or contemporary situation. Sometimes it is easier for students to express ideas when they can speak through the mouth of a puppet than if they have to portray the character themselves.

An easy, quick way to make puppets is to draw faces of characters on the bottom folded side of a paper bag with the mouth on the fold.

Example: Use paper bag puppets to reenact the wedding feast at Cana told about in John 2:1-11. (*Bible Exploration*)

Or, use paper bag puppets to resolve the situation presented in your group's open-ended story. (*Life Exploration*)

Plays

There are a number of good plays available for youth to plan and present. Some require only two people, while others require crowds of youth to participate. A good play presentation requires careful planning and enough time for preparation.

Play Reading

Not every play must be a production. Sometimes parts of plays can be used simply by having members of the group read the parts for the large group audience. The departmental leader could introduce the part of the play being presented, giving background material for the scene to be read.

This type of presentation does not require rehearsals, although a once-through reading before the meeting is suggested. Staging, costumes and lighting are unnecesary. And acting skill is not required of the readers.

Scenes from secular plays can be used to illustrate a point in the learning experience of the group.

Similar to play reading is *conversational Scripture*. This is used with narrative passages of Scripture, especially in the Gospels, or in the Old Testament narratives. Different parts of the narrative are assigned to readers. The passage is then read as though it were a play. This is done by leaving out the "and he said,..." from the conversation. This helps to bring the passage to life as it makes the interaction between characters clear.

Roleplay

This is a special type of drama which is especially effective with youth. A roleplay is a brief, unrehearsed presentation of a real life situation by two or three students while the rest of the group observes. This method especially deals with the "feeling" area of learning.

This method has tremendous value when used correctly and with a clear objective in mind. A great deal of Christian truth involves relationships—how we are to treat one another because we know and love God through Jesus Christ. Roleplay deals with relationships, and can help apply, crystallize and bring to life spiritual principles as no other method can.

First a problem is presented to the group. It might be an open-ended story with the ending to be acted out, a biblical story or a modern parallel to a biblical situation.

Once the problem is presented, actors are chosen. (Care must be exercised in not giving an unpopular person the unpopular role.) Names are given the actors, and some brief instructions could be given either individually or to the group of actors. There is no rehearsal, but a few moments are given to allow the actors time to "psych" themselves up for the role.

The actual roleplay should not be too long, running from one to five minutes. The number of participants should seldom be more than three; two is ideal. It is the teacher's responsibility to make sure each actor knows what is expected of him in his role.

After the roleplay the class discusses what happened, the feelings involved, and alternate ways the situation could have been handled.

Example: In the parable of the prodigal son, the teacher might focus on the attitude of the elder brother. After describing his bitterness and self-pity, three "actors" would be chosen, one to play the part of the father, one the prodigal, and the other the elder son. The setting would be the next day, when the three meet and begin discussing the welcome home feast the night before.

From that point on, the "actors" are on their own. The conversation is imaginary, but helps the learners get into the feelings of the characters. (*Bible Exploration*)

Another example is a problem between a son and his father. The father could be really angry because he does not want to let his "irresponsible" son use the car. The son needs the car and wants to convince his father that he will be responsible and can be trusted. (*Life Exploration*)

The leader stops the roleplay when the point has been made and emotions are still actively involved. The roleplay should not continue beyond the climactic point of the situation.

Remember, following the presentation, the group discusses what has been acted out and suggests strengths and weaknesses in the solutions presented. This discussion is important in making the roleplay a good learning experience. If there is interest, the scene might be repeated with different actors involved.

The evaluation should include debriefing the actors, asking them why they did what they did and how they felt about their role. Listening teams might be assigned to "feel with" an individual actor and to be prepared to discuss why they reacted as they did in the roleplay. During evaluation and discussion, the assigned names should be used rather than the person's real name.

Roleplay Adaptation

Divide the large group into two or three groups and have each group represent one of the people in a Bible situation. They do not act out the situation, but instead attempt to feel how the person might have felt and then give reasons for what they would do in the situation and why. This technique is good for students who are too shy to actually roleplay the situation.

Example: In the parable of the good Samaritan, one group would represent the priest, another group would be the Levite, and the third group would be the good Samaritan. Individual members of each group are then asked to explain why they behaved as they did in the parable. (*Bible Exploration*)

■ ART

Not everyone is an artist, obviously, but youth enjoy working with their hands in various art projects. Furthermore, many students are visually oriented and "seeing" helps them remember important points longer. Moreover the struggle to express ideas visually forces students to evaluate essential ideas carefully.

There are several art forms which can be used with youth which will get them involved in the learning process. The objective in each case is to encourage your learners to express their learning and ideas in some art form. Reassure them that "fancy" or "polished" art is not the object of a Bible learning method, but that communicating truth and ideas is the important thing.

Coat of Arms

Although a coat of arms is the end product, the value of having learners design symbols for a coat of arms is in the thinking and discussion required to crystallize the main ideas into a drawing.

Example: Draw a shield on a piece of poster paper. Divide the surface into four quadrants. In the first quadrant draw a symbol representing David; in the second a symbol representing his sin; in the third a symbol representing Nathan's message; and in the fourth a symbol representing the consequences. (See 2 Samuel 11:1-12:14.) (*Bible Exploration*)

Collage

A montage using objects, cloth, and other materials as well as paper. (See Montage.)

Drawings and Doodles

Drawings can be done in small groups, each with an appointed artist. The artist listens to the ideas of the group members and creates a drawing that suggests their combined ideas. He then explains the drawing to the other groups.

Doodles can be a fun way of expressing feelings. Artistic talent is not required, only the willingness to move a pencil with feeling. Each group member is asked to try to enter into the feeling of the narrative in Scripture and express it in a doodle.

Example: The real value of doodles comes in explaining them to the rest of the group, describing how they express the feelings in the passage of Scripture. Try to feel like Mary and Martha as Jesus comes four days too late to heal Lazarus. How did they feel when they saw Jesus coming? Then how did they feel after Jesus brought Lazarus back from the dead? Try to doodle one or two drawings that express these feelings. (*Bible Exploration*)

Graffiti

A phrase such as "Happiness Is..." or "Thanks, Lord, for..." is written at the top of chalkboard or a large sheet of newsprint or shelf paper. As learners arrive, they are given chalk, pencils or felt pens and encouraged to write or draw whatever they feel is appropriate to the theme suggested by the heading. (Graffiti usually makes a good Approach.)

Jeremiah Graph

This is a graph which charts a person's "ups" and "downs."

Example: Based on the events in Judges 6 and 7, on a scale of 1–10 chart Gideon's confidence in God's ability to help him complete the task during that period of time. *(Bible Exploration)*

FIGURE 2

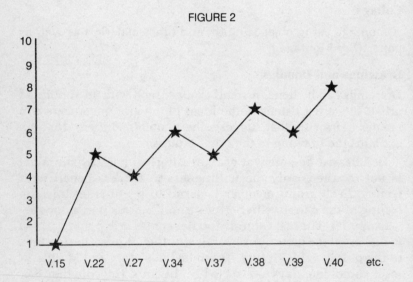

Note: The reason it is called a "Jeremiah" graph is because Jeremiah experienced so many ups and downs in his own life.

Mobile

A mobile is composed of strips or pieces of paper, wire, or plastic straws, etc., in balance with each other and is usually suspended from a wall, ceiling, etc., so that the various parts may shift in the currents of air.

Example: Make a mobile based on Galatians 5:22,23. Each shape should represent one of the fruits of the Spirit, such as a heart for love, etc. *(Bible Exploration)*

Montage

A montage is the combination of several distinct pictures to make a composite picture on a single theme. These are fun to make and are often very revealing about the needs and interests of the youth. Group members can work individually or in small groups. Be sure you have enough room for them to spread out their clippings.

You will need to provide a large piece of butcher paper or poster paper for each montage. Assign members of the group the task of bringing stacks of old magazines, preferably the picture type. You will need a pair of scissors for each person (or you could tear pictures), glue and felt pens.

Your learners should skim through the magazines looking for pictures and captions which express their feelings about an assigned subject. Many teachers prefer to give students a box of pre-selected pictures to select from as this prevents distractions caused by pictures inappropriate for the class discussion.

This can also be a project done at home and then brought to class. Part of the learning experience comes as each student is given opportunity to explain the meaning of his montage to the others in the group. Montage assignments are usually used during *Life Exploration*.

Example: A group of junior highs were asked to create a montage that expressed their answer to the question, "Who am I?" The results were in some cases superficial, but in others, showed a depth of expression.

Paper Tear

Ask learners to select a piece of colored paper and tear a shape which reminds them of some idea (for example, the results or benefits of salvation). You may need to suggest several possible shapes to help them get started. Allow about two minutes for thinking and tearing. Then ask learners to share briefly in twos or threes what they tore and why (for example, flames for salvation from hell, a broken chain for freedom from sin, a heart for

God's love). If time permits, after small group sharing, ask several volunteers to share with the entire class. This technique could be used in any part of the session depending on how it is used.

Posters

Posters will have as many uses as your imagination will allow. Here are a few examples:

Based on Numbers 13, you have been commissioned by Joshua and Caleb to create a travel poster to encourage the Israelites to enter the Promised Land. (*Bible Exploration*)

Illustrate the objects of Jesus' temptation in Matthew 4. (*Bible Exploration*)

Illustrate temptations young people face today. (*Life Exploration*)

Illustrate advantages of being a Christian. (*Life Exploration*)

Time Line

A time line can be used for an overview or review of a sequence of events, where the learners work together to organize the information. A time line can be made on a piece of shelf paper. A second possibility is to suspend a clothesline and clip colored papers to the line to represent different events. A third way is to give each student a card marked with an event (or person) and ask them to line themselves up in sequential order. (*Bible Exploration*)

Word Picture

A word poster is a collection of words cut or torn out of newspapers or magazines which are glued on to a poster board in a meaningful shape which communicates the focus of their research.

Example: A word poster on the Holy Spirit might include words such as comfort, power, inside out, breath of God, etc. These words could be arranged and glued on the poster board in the shape of a dove, column of flame or cross. (*Bible or Life Exploration*)

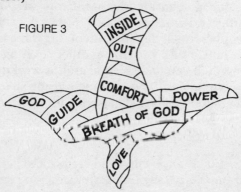

FIGURE 3

Write-on Slides

A slide presentation may be prepared in class through the use of write-on slides. Students draw pictures or words on write-on slides (Kodak Ectagraphic Write-On Slides obtainable at camera stores) using overhead transparency pens. These usually illustrate Bible or contemporary stories.

Examples: Ask each group to read James 2:14-26 together, looking for the highlights of James' message in this section. Then the group is to prepare six slides and a written narration which summarize the message of the section. They may use symbols, pictures or words on their slides to visualize the narration. Their narration can be selected phrases or verses from the text, an original narration, a combination of the two, or even poetry. They should plan their presentation to last two to three minutes.

Allow 10 minutes for reading and planning, and 10 to 15 minutes to make their slides and write their narration. Notify them to begin making their slides and when 5 minutes remain, and then 1 minute remains for work. (*Bible Exploration*)

Or, use the slides to illustrate how a junior higher can show love to his/her parents. (*Life Exploration*)

■ MUSIC

Music has long played an important role in communicating spiritual truths and worshiping God. Music is very much a part of young people's life-style today. Involving them in Bible learning through music will provide another exciting stimulus for spiritual growth. If you have several groups working on projects and one involves music, have the music group share last and ask the entire class to sing along. This will add special emphasis and enthusiasm to your lesson.

Add a Verse

Have learners take an established hymn and write one more verse based on the passage of Scripture being studied. When preparing to write lyrics, it is usually best to jot down several expressions of the main ideas you wish to communicate to get started. This generally breaks the ice. Moreover, while ideas for song lyrics sometimes come slowly at first, they often pick up speed later like a snowball rolling downhill and finish in a flurry of excitement.

Here is an extra verse to "Trust and Obey" written after studying about Jonah.

Jonah knew what to do
for the Lord told him to.
But he disobeyed and ran away

Took a trip on a ship
The result was a dip
In the water where he thought he'd stay.

(Bible Exploration)

Musical Commercial

This is variation of "Add a Verse" or "Songwriting."

Example: Ananias has asked you to write a musical commercial to convince the Christians in Damascus that Saul is indeed a Christian (see Acts 9:1-22). *(Bible Exploration)*

Paraphrase Hymn Lyrics

This is similar to paraphrasing Scripture. Students write the song thoughts in their own words. The result is to be read, not sung.

Example:

Hymn	**Paraphrase**
He leadeth me	He leads me
O blessed thought	Far out thought

(Life Exploration)

Song Comparison

Learners compare secular songs with either Christian songs or Scripture.

Example: Compare a modern love song with 1 Corinthians 13:4-7. What similarities and differences do you see? *(Life Exploration)*

Songwriting

Writing a new song or new words to an old song can be a stimulating and exciting experience. Some groups may find it difficult at first, but when a finished product is presented, it usually amazes them. Songs do much to reinforce Bible truths and concepts.

Example: When one junior high group was challenged to write a song about their relationship to Jesus, they picked "Yankee Doodle" for their tune and wrote:

Jesus is my Lord and Saviour and He loves me *so.*
He will always be my *guide* everywhere I go.
Chorus:
Praise His name I love Him *so.*
    Oh, praise His name forever.
Praise His name, I love Him *so.*
    Jesus Christ my Saviour.

Verse 2:
When I talk to Him in prayer and read His Word to know.
I learn to love Him more and more, and in His image grow.
Verse 3:
As I walk along life's road I never need to fear,
For I know from God's Word, that He is always near.
(*Life Exploration*)

■ LECTURE[1]

Is the lecture a good Bible learning method? Yes. However, to be effective, the lecture should be used selectively and for a definite purpose. Take a look at the content of the lesson you plan to teach. Can the material be discovered by students, or must it be explained? Is there a lot of material to cover, such as in a survey course? Do the learners need a broad overview of ideas or events? Is the information technical? If any of these questions can be answered yes, the lecture may be the method you should use.

Preparing a Lecture

Once you have decided to use the lecture, gather sufficient material to make the lecture interesting. Use your teacher's manual, Bible dictionaries and commentaries, relevant magazine and newspaper articles and other appropriate material. Then organize your main ideas. Remember, even though you are lecturing you still need to select one focus and determine your objectives. Then prepare an outline listing the main points and the sub-points. (Do not try to cover too many points in one lesson.) Build upon what your learners know—progress from the known to the unknown. Add illustrations, maps, charts and other visuals to help clarify the points.

Practice your lecture at home before you present it to the class. Stand in front of a mirror as you talk to see how you appear. Do you slump, lean over the podium, pace back and forth, or move around nervously? Tape the lecture and listen to yourself. Or tape a class session and listen to it at home. How do you sound? Do you speak clearly and distinctly? Or do you slur your words, punctuate your lesson frequently with uhs and ahs or with a favorite, but annoying, expression such as "you know," or "know what I mean?"

Some teachers have had their session videotaped, then listened to and watched themselves in action. These teachers confessed that it was a difficult and painful experience, but most beneficial and they wanted to do it again.

Presenting a Lecture

When you present your lecture, use language your learners will understand. A wise speech teacher once said, "If you can't say it simply, you don't really understand it." So say it simply and effectively. If your class is full of PhD's you can get away with a few six-syllable words. But for the most part, stick to simple words that everyone can understand. Vary the pitch of your voice and the rate of speed at which you speak to emphasize a change in ideas.

Learners learn more and remember more when they have opportunity to respond to a lecture. During a lecture your learners can—

- Take notes.
- Complete a work sheet giving a brief outline of the lecture.
- Serve as listening teams and listen for answers to questions given them before the lecture begins.
- Take an inventory test before the lecture begins to start them thinking about the subject.
- Summarize the lecture with the person sitting next to them during the last five minutes of the session.

Vary your method of presenting the lecture. For example, you can—

- State the main concept or thought of the session.
- Ask learners to read the concept from a chart.

- Ask learners to reword the concept.
- Present the necessary information, then give a brief demonstration.
- Tape the material prior to the class and play it during class time.
- List the main ideas of the lecture on index cards and distribute these to learners as they arrive; when you reach a particular point in the lecture, ask the person who has that card to read it aloud.

Increasing Retantion Through Review

Repetition is essential in any type of learning situation. Unfortunately, we forget a great deal of what we hear. To help your learners remember what they have heard in a lecture you can—

- Review part of the content at the end or some other appropriate spot in the lecture.
- Use charts to review material.
- Summarize occasionally.
- Distribute or display an outline for continual review.
- Ask your learners to summarize the lecture or part of it.
- Assign research projects and outside reading on the lecture topic.
- Ask questions and give tests.

A lecture should *always* be accompanied by some kind of visual aid. In most lectures hearing is the only sense used. Yet we also learn through our other four senses.

Several studies have indicated that the greatest degree of learning and retention takes place when visuals accompany a lecture.

A wide variety of visual teaching tools is available today —charts, maps, lines, diagrams, pictures, the overhead projector, films and filmstrips. Their use is limited only by your imagination.

Create a climate for learning. The arrangement of the chairs, temperature of the room and your attitude and friendliness (or lack of it) toward your learners will aid or detract from your lecture.

Want to be a really good lecturer? Then you must continually work at both the content and presentation of your lectures. Your presentation should be well done, but the focal point of the class must be the Word of God—not you.

▪ CONSIDER AUDIOVISUALS

Often teachers think of audiovisual aids as aids to the teacher, and that to make extensive use of them is somehow an admission that "I must be a weak teacher if I need audiovisuals to get my point across." Others have seen audiovisuals as "frills" that take too much time to prepare.

We really need to see that audiovisuals are a help to the learner, and that good audiovisuals make a strong teacher's teaching even stronger.

Audiovisuals illustrate and reinforce ideas, facts, concepts, events, stories, themes and principles. They aid memorization. They provoke learners to apply scriptural principles in contemporary living. The more a learner can see the more we can expect him to remember.

Visuals and audiovisuals not only increase retention, but they can also be used to increase our understanding. One teacher of junior highers relates the following:

"It wasn't until I saw the two posters side by side that it really hit me. One group prepared a poster of the serpent in the wilderness from John 3:14a during our Bible study while a second group prepared a poster of Jesus on the cross, based on John 3:14b. Suddenly I understood what Jesus was saying to Nicodemus. 'Nick, you don't have it put together yet. But when you see me on the cross, remember the bronze serpent and you will know who I am and why I came.' And I remembered it was at the cross when most of Jesus' followers were deserting Him, that Nicodemus declared himself. He went to Pilate, asked for Jesus' body, and helped Joseph of Arimathea prepare it for burial. I don't believe I would have discovered that if I hadn't seen those two posters side by side as we were studying that passage!"

When visuals are combined with the audio, retention soars much higher. A perfect example of this level of input would be a film or a TV presentation. ("No wonder they remember their favorite TV programs better than my lectures!")

Visuals include maps, charts, bulletins, pamphlets, flipcharts, posters, banners, photographs, displays, chalkboard writing, pocket charts, flannelboards, models, slides and overhead transparencies. Audio aids include records, cassette tapes, etc. Audiovisual combinations include filmstrips, videotapes, movies and slide-tape shows.

A teacher using audiovisuals for the first time will want to learn the mechanics of the equipment so that the learning experience goes smoothly during the session. Be sure to check the equipment each time you plan to use it for a session. Unfortunately, most of us teachers remember at least one experience when something went wrong. Either the motion picture projector would not thread properly, a bulb was burned out on the overhead projector or a power cord was missing. While our learners waited and fidgeted, we fumed and threw up our hands in frustration.

However, don't let the extra preparation required for the use of audiovisual equipment keep you from using it as often as appropriate. It is more than worth the extra effort.

Audiovisuals not readily available can be prepared by either the teacher or the learners. The learners can pre-record needed tape, music or narratives. They can prepare slide presentations and some even have access to equipment for making home movies. These audiovisuals may be less than professional in artistic quality, but the personal investment on the part of the learners making them will make them very worthwhile.

When we think of audiovisuals as an aid to the learner rather than as an aid to the teacher, we will be more likely to make

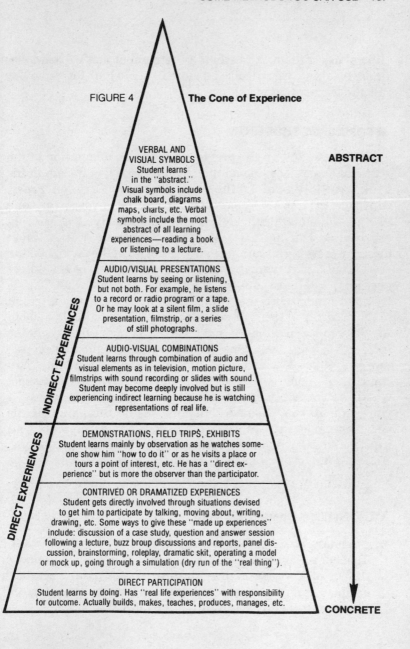

FIGURE 4   **The Cone of Experience**

VERBAL AND VISUAL SYMBOLS
Student learns in the "abstract." Visual symbols include chalk board, diagrams maps, charts, etc. Verbal symbols include the most abstract of all learning experiences—reading a book or listening to a lecture.

AUDIO/VISUAL PRESENTATIONS
Student learns by seeing or listening, but not both. For example, he listens to a record or radio program or a tape. Or he may look at a silent film, a slide presentation, filmstrip, or a series of still photographs.

AUDIO-VISUAL COMBINATIONS
Student learns through combination of audio and visual elements as in television, motion picture, filmstrips with sound recording or slides with sound. Student may become deeply involved but is still experiencing indirect learning because he is watching representations of real life.

DEMONSTRATIONS, FIELD TRIPS, EXHIBITS
Student learns mainly by observation as he watches someone show him "how to do it" or as he visits a place or tours a point of interest, etc. He has a "direct experience" but is more the observer than the participator.

CONTRIVED OR DRAMATIZED EXPERIENCES
Student gets directly involved through situations devised to get him to participate by talking, moving about, writing, drawing, etc. Some ways to give these "made up experiences" include: discussion of a case study, question and answer session following a lecture, buzz group discussions and reports, panel discussion, brainstorming, roleplay, dramatic skit, operating a model or mock up, going through a simulation (dry run of the "real thing").

DIRECT PARTICIPATION
Student learns by doing. Has "real life experiences" with responsibility for outcome. Actually builds, makes, teaches, produces, manages, etc.

ABSTRACT

CONCRETE

INDIRECT EXPERIENCES

DIRECT EXPERIENCES

liberal use of them. And when we remember that we learn even more by doing, we will also be more likely to look for audiovisuals the learners can make.

■ SOME LAST THOUGHTS

The illustration on the previous page is an adaptation of the "cone of experience" developed by educator Edgar Dale in his book, *Audio-Visual Methods in Teaching* (Dryden Press, copyright 1954, p. 43). According to Dale, the lower on the cone you go, the more direct, purposeful and effective the learning experience can be. Dale stresses, however, that in most teaching-learning situations many, if not all of the factors on the cone, play a part. Verbal symbols, for example, are absolutely necessary to almost any teaching situation. But what Dale is trying to emphasize is that verbal symbols alone leave the lesson in the category of the indirect and unreal. A great deal of teaching done today in public schools as well as in churches is in the indirect category. Even the effective medium of the motion picture is indirect. We learn best, however, when we actually "try something—when we get our teeth into an assignment or project where we are responsible for the outcome." In other words, if your students can "take part" in your lessons through methods and techniques such as discussion, case study, roleplay, field trips, making and operating models, going through simulations, etc., your lessons will be more real to them because you will be using a more direct method of teaching.

FOOTNOTE ■ Chapter Eleven

1. Norman Wright, "Talk! Talk! Talk!," *Sunday School Teacher's Planbook—Youth*, (Glendale, CA: Regal Books, 1975), p. 2. Some of the ideas presented here have been adapted from the book, *Using the Lecture in Teaching and Training* by LeRoy Ford, (Broadman Press).

Does It Work?

Does this kind of teaching bring lasting results? When a Sunday School teacher was asked this question, he replied, "Since we have begun to teach this way, I have seen young people who were turned off to Bible study come alive and bring their friends to share. I have seen young people who were rebellious toward God and parents over a period of time voluntarily submit to both after wrestling with God's Word in an open atmosphere where honesty was not only permitted but encouraged. I have heard parents say, 'I don't know what you are doing differently but keep it up. The changes at home are super!' I have watched them becoming mature sons and daughters of God as they have taken responsibility for their learning and have become doers of the Word. Does it last? Yes! Yes! Yes!"

May God encourage your heart as you lead your learners in these same paths.

Suggested Reading

Brown, Lowell E., with Reed, Bobbie. *Your Sunday School Can Grow*. Glendale, CA: Regal, 1974.

Dale, Edgar, *Audio-Visual Methods in Teaching*. Hinsdale, IL: Dryden Press, 1954.

De Jong, Arthur J. *Making It to Adulthood: The Emerging Self*. Philadelphia, PA: Westminster, 1972.

Erikson, Erik H. *Youth Identity and Crisis*. New York, NY: W. W. Norton & Co., 1968.

Ezell, Mancil. *Youth in Bible Study*. Nashville, TN: Convention Press, 1970.

Gesell, Arnold; Ilg, Frances L.; and Ames, Louis B. *Youth: The Years from Ten to Sixteen*. New York, NY: Harper and Row, 1956.

Ginott, Haim G. *Between Parent and Teenager*. New York, NY: Macmillan Co., 1969.

Horne, Herman H. *Teaching Techniques of Jesus*. Grand Rapids, MI: Kregel, 1971.

Joy, Donald M. *Meaningful Learning in the Church*. Winona Lake, IN: Light and Life Press, 1969.

Leypoldt, Martha M. *40 Ways to Teach in Groups*. Valley Forge, PA: Judson, 1967.

Leypoldt, Martha M. *Learning Is Change*. Valley Forge, PA: Judson, 1971.

Mager, Robert F. *Developing Attitude Toward Learning*. Palo Alto, CA: Fearon, 1968.

Mayle, Peter. *What's Happening to Me?* Secaucus, NJ: Lyle Stuart Inc., 1975.

Reed, C. Edward. *Sunday School Teacher's Planbook—Youth*. Glendale, CA: Regal, 1975.

Richards, Lawrence O. *Youth Ministry*. Grand Rapids, MI: Zondervan, 1972.

Strommen, Merton P. *Five Cries of Youth*. New York, NY: Harper & Row, 1974.

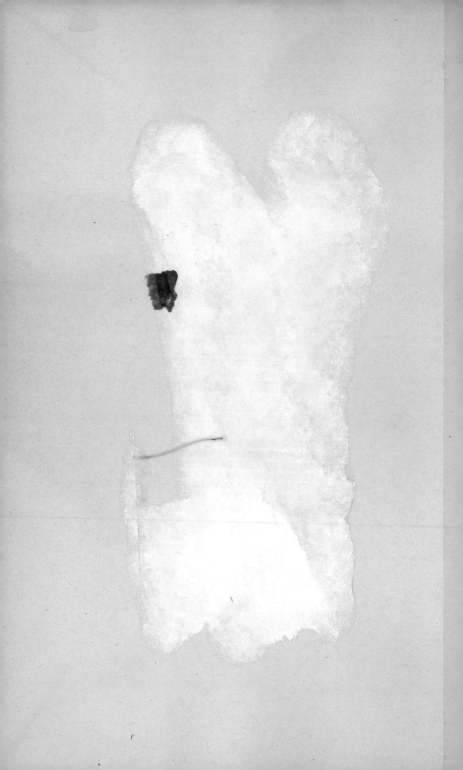